'What a wonderful story of Bhaskar, a devout and dedicated Hindu, who spent years searching for the meaning of life. Finally, he met a Christian who was instrumental in leading him to Jesus Christ – the one who is "the way, the truth and the life". How many of us would be willing to give up friends and family to follow our Lord Jesus Christ, as Bhaskar did? It is my great pleasure to recommend this touching and powerful book. You will be inspired and challenged as you read it.'

Maud Kells OBE, WEC International missionary in DR Congo for 50 years and author of *An Open Door*

'A fascinating insight into a very different world and world view and a wonderful reminder of the power of the gospel to transform the lives of people from any background. After reading this book I felt better informed about Hinduism and more motivated to share the gospel in my multi-cultural community.'

Clare Heath-Whyte, St Lawrence, Morden, writer and speaker

'In Brahmin Reborn, *Esther Sandys gives us a fascinating window into the inner workings of Hinduism. Through the story of her father-in-law, Bhaskar, she paints a clear picture of the difference between Hinduism and Christianity and of one man's transition from or engagingly written, this book and encourage your faith.'

D1419842

Jean Gibsor

BRAHMIN
REBORN

BRAHMIN REBORN

publishing

BRAHMIN REBORN

BHASKAR SREERANGAM

WITH ESTHER SANDYS

Unless otherwise stated, Scripture quotations are taken from The Holy Bible, New International Version (Anglicised Edition). Copyright © 1979, 1984, 2011 by Biblica (formerly International Bible Society). Used by permission of Hodder & Stoughton Publishers. All rights reserved. 'NIV' is a registered trademark of Biblica. UK trademark number 1448790.

Copyright © 2019 by Esther Sandys

First published in Great Britain in 2019

The right of Esther Sandys to be identified as the Author of this Work has been asserted by her in accordance with the Copyright, Designs and Patents Act 1988.

All rights reserved. No part of this publication may be reproduced, stored in a retrieval system or transmitted in any form or by any means, electronic, mechanical, photocopying, recording or otherwise, without the prior permission of the publisher or the Copyright Licensing Agency.

British Library Cataloguing in Publication Data
A record for this book is available from the British Library

ISBN: 978-1-913278-04-5

Designed and typeset by Pete Barnsley (CreativeHoot.com)

Printed in Denmark by Nørhaven

10Publishing, a division of 10ofthose.com
Unit C, Tomlinson Road, Leyland, PR25 2DY, England

Email: info@10ofthose.com
Website: www.10ofthose.com

1 3 5 7 10 8 6 4 2

Now this is eternal life: that they know you, the only true God, and Jesus Christ, whom you have sent.

(John 17:3)

DEDICATION

To dear Bharathi, Krishna, Prasad, Prabha and Mohan:
there were many motivations to write my story but
primary among them was my long-standing, heartfelt
desire that you would understand how I was led by grace
to Jesus, and that you yourselves may believe that Jesus
is the Christ, the Son of God, and that by believing you
may have life in His name.

To Suren, my life partner and co-worker for the Lord:
you are a pure diamond, consistently combining faith
with action.

Finally, to my three children and eight grandchildren: you
are a constant reminder that God's faithfulness endures
from generation to generation.

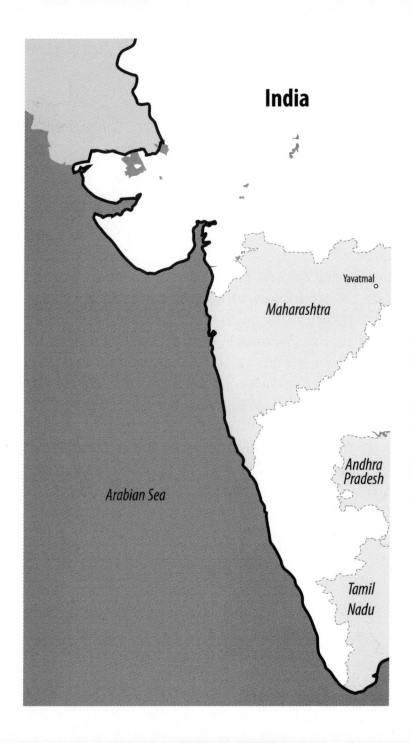

CONTENTS

ACKNOWLEDGEMENTS

ACKNOWLEDGEMENTS

We are truly grateful for the support and encouragement of many people throughout this project and for all those who, over decades, have asked when Bhaskar's story will be published, thus motivating us to persevere.

There are, naturally, certain individuals for whom we are especially thankful. From very early on, when we were transcribing cassette-tape recordings (remember those?), Joy Sandys literally stepped in with her foot pedal and super-efficient typing skills to speed up an otherwise tedious and disheartening process. She also read and helpfully commented on several drafts. Thank you, Mum!

In what turned out to be Bhaskar's last year with us here, Surendri Sreerangam encouraged us and facilitated our time together so that we could enjoy deep and enriching conversation. She took care of all the household duties so that we could immerse ourselves in the 1960s and 70s, grappling with memories, cross-cultural understandings and turns of phrase. Thank you, Mummy!

To our four readers, Carole, Michael, Paul and Tarun: thank you for giving up your time to read the text. Your thoughtful and wise comments have helped shape the narrative and encouraged us that the book could be understood and even enjoyed.

To the professionals who have had a huge – and godly – influence on the final structure and tenor of the book: it would be nowhere near as accessible or readable as it is without your insights and wise (albeit sometimes painful) suggestions. Thank you, Ali Hull, for giving us hope. Thank you, Julie Hatherall, for your meticulous and sensitive editing and collaboration. Jonathan Carswell and Lois Ferguson at 10ofThose, thank you for your positivity and implementation.

Shalom, Rohan and Asha: you have constantly encouraged, prayed for, read and reread the umpteen drafts that have culminated in these pages. Thank you for being kind and sensitive.

Ultimately, we give thanks and praise to our gracious heavenly Father, without whom there would be no book and, moreover, no story to tell.

PROLOGUE

... ask and it will be given to you; seek and you will find; knock and the door will be opened to you. For everyone who asks receives; the one who seeks finds; and to the one who knocks, the door will be opened.

(Luke 11:9–10)

Everything else had failed. All my efforts to find the answer to my agonising question had come to nothing. It was time to give the Hindu gods an ultimatum: 'If you don't tell me tonight how I can come to you in heaven when I die, tomorrow I will kill myself.' I wholeheartedly addressed this passionate plea to whichever of my gods were listening. I was deadly serious.

To be honest, I wasn't the slightest bit keen on the prospect. But neither could I keep going with the desperate hunger for answers that had been eating away at me for over half my life. I wanted to know how to avoid being born again and again in cycles of reincarnation. I didn't want to keep coming back to this earth, time after time, never reaching paradise with Brahman, the 'supreme (or ultimate) reality'. Having interrogated family members, priests and the gods themselves, I was at my wits' end at how I could receive release from these dreaded multiple lives. I could no longer conceive of carrying on my life without the guarantee that all my religious devotion would pay off. Where was the hope that I longed for? Where was the peace that I craved?

I believed the deities would be profoundly upset when they saw that a follower as great as me was going to die. I thought that they would do something out of desperation to save me from the slow and painful death I'd planned. Surely they would provide the answer I so needed? I wasn't asking for fame and fortune, or a golden ticket to heaven. I was just asking for information. Having been used to supernatural happenings throughout my life, I fully expected a prompt, dramatic reply. I believed that it was entirely possible that one of the thousands – no, millions – of gods I followed as a Hindu might be able to respond to my cry.

So, having made my suicidal ultimatum, I waited patiently. All night, I waited with bated breath.

But by the break of dawn, to my dismay and despite my expectations, nothing at all had happened.

Conditioned by years of religious practices, still I waited, with an unshakeable belief that I'd be answered: maybe with a light; possibly with a voice; perhaps by an appearance. I would even have been satisfied with a fellow human being delivering a personal message to me.

But no such thing happened. Nobody answered. No god I'd known came to my rescue there in the Indian city of Madras. So started Saturday 10 September 1966: the day I was going to kill myself.

1

MY FAMILY

My story really begins – as most people's do – even before I was born, in the 1910s. Hope and excitement were brewing for a priestly Hindu family on the south-east coast of India. Suryanaraya Rambhatla (my grandfather) had had two unsuccessful marriages: both his first and second wives had died. While this is tragic for any husband, it was disastrous for him: as a Hindu man, he had been taught that his entire eternity depended on having children. Yet Suryanaraya made a subsequent match with a girl from the well-reputed Sreerangam family. Everyone expected it to be 'third time lucky'. Both families had a similar education, wealth and conservative attitude. In time, this couple were indeed blessed with four children. But while awaiting the birth of their fifth child, Suryanaraya unexpectedly died. This left his wife, who I would later call Ammamma, a widow at the age of thirty, with four children to care for and a baby on the way.

The hunt for husbands

The years went by and Ammamma needed to find good husbands for her three daughters. For Hindus, the first criterion for a good husband is that he must come from a 'good' family, that is a respectable one. Conveniently, this can be learnt largely by their surname, which implies not only that the person is a Hindu, but also which caste (section of society) and sub-caste they are from and their geographical place of origin.

To properly understand Hinduism and the way it affects people's day-to-day lives, you need to understand this caste system and the inflexible influence it brings to all relationships, especially marriages. The concept comes from the Hindu scriptures known as the *Laws of Manu*. All human beings are divided into four hierarchical groups at birth, called castes. These four divisions, from top to bottom, are: Brahmins (priests), Kshatriyas (royals or warriors), Vaishyas (professionals) and Sudras (servants). Sudras can be subdivided into two further classes, servants and untouchables, though this distinction is a grey area. The untouchables are also referred to as Dalits.

The caste system is completely rigid: a person is born into a caste, and there is absolutely nothing she or he can do to change that in this present life. That caste is both determined by someone's good or bad actions in their previous incarnation and governed by the caste of their parents, particularly their father. The caste system then determines a person's entire social structure: identity, friends, career and spouse. Anyone who breaks the expectations of their caste is seen as a deviant, and will return as a lower caste in their next incarnation.

What is right or wrong is determined by each caste's customs and cultures. For example, Brahmins, Kshatriyas and Vaishyas are allowed to go into all places of Hindu worship, whereas Sudras are not permitted to enter any. However, only Brahmins are allowed into the inner sanctuary of a Hindu temple. Brahmins aren't allowed to work with leather (because the cow is a sacred animal in Hinduism), but people from the other castes can. So although castes may appear similar to social classes in westernised societies, they are more rigid and clearly defined.

The second consideration for a good Hindu marriage is the horoscope of both the husband- and wife-to-be. This is not simply something published on the twelve signs of the zodiac. For a Hindu, the horoscope is much more specific, taking into account the year, date and hour of birth, in conjunction with the positions of the planets at that precise time in history. Drawn up by a priest when a child is born, it also makes statements, albeit vague ones, about the baby's future, such as their life expectancy, highest anticipated level of education and prospects of wealth. Both the man's and the woman's personal horoscopes have to 'match' if they are to be allowed to get married. Even the date of the wedding will be set by their horoscopes.

The third factor in a Hindu marriage is a dowry (marriage settlement). The dowry given depends on each family's circumstances, as well as on the expectations of those receiving it. However, a dowry usually consists of gifts of gold, silver, furniture, clothing and money. Furthermore, the ability to give a good dowry is usually a major factor in the choice of Hindu marriage partners (although it's by no means unique to Hinduism or even India).[1]

Venkamma

Having taken into account all these aspects, Ammamma identified a suitable Sreerangam husband for Venkamma, the oldest of her daughters. Venkamma was engaged at a young age, as was the Hindu custom in those days. She had no influence on the choice of her life partner and wouldn't even meet her husband until the day of their wedding. Once Venkamma reached physical maturity, all the wedding rituals were conducted. The correct 'auspicious' time and date were set for the wedding. Clothes and sweets were sent to the relatives. Venkamma was decorated with a red, silk sari, as well as with flowers and jewellery. She was escorted by her close relatives to her husband's home and to the decorated room where they would start their married life together.

All this is intimidating for any young bride. However, it was worse for Venkamma: the day that was designed to be full of celebration actually became a cursed day of mourning. Instead of her husband coming home triumphantly to his young bride, news arrived that he had suddenly died. A few hours later, his dead body followed.

This was a tragedy, but especially for Venkamma. Without exception, everyone blamed her for his death, saying that she had caused it by her bad deeds, or karma, in her previous incarnations. Since Venkamma became a widow at such a young age, they concluded she must be a cursed troublemaker who had accumulated very bad karma. The in-laws were bitter and furious that the moment their daughter-in-law had stepped into their house, their beloved son had died. They therefore called Venkamma's mother to say they didn't want this disgrace of a girl, along with her bad karma, to reside with them.

Thus Venkamma, who had left her maternal home as a resplendent bride, now had to return there wreathed in white, the Indian colour of mourning. She had been given a shameful bare head, along with a disgrace that she would never shake off until she herself faced the funeral pyre.

Even to this day, arranged marriages are conducted in millions of homes around India (and indeed the world). Many widows end up in the same tragic situation as Venkamma. In Hinduism, becoming a widow before bearing children has, for millennia, been completely unforgiveable and therefore is social death.[2] Perhaps it is not surprising that such women often commit suicide, preferring to face instant death than a lifetime of social torture.

Ramana

Despite the apparently cursed first Sreerangam–Rambhatla match, Ammamma's second daughter, Ramana, nevertheless married another member of the

Sreerangam family: Surya, who was a teacher and fanatical religious man. For example, he would take a ceremonial bath several times a day and wouldn't let himself come into contact with anything 'unclean' from the outside world. Ammamma and the whole family considered Surya to be a nuisance, to say the least.

Ten long years passed by and still Ramana and Surya had no children. Neighbours and relatives repeatedly questioned them as to why Ramana hadn't become pregnant, while secretly holding on to their belief that, as a barren woman, Ramana must have lived a shameful life in a previous incarnation. Note the sheer bias, utterly engrained in Hindu thinking, that childlessness is the 'fault' of the woman. Of course, at that time medical interventions were nowhere near as advanced as they are now, and neither was people's understanding of the facts of life. Ramana and Surya waited and waited for their longed-for child, becoming increasingly frustrated in the process, as well as facing shame and ostracism from the community.

Ammamma now had two disgraced daughters. What would be the outcome for Ratnam, her youngest daughter?

Ratnam

Ratnam (or 'Bucchi'), who was to become my mother, was beautiful. In fact, her family considered her to be so beautiful that they wouldn't let her go near the windows at home. Like many Hindus, they believed that *nazar* (the 'evil eye', a kind of magic) would put a curse on anything attractive, so they 'hid' Bucchi indoors for most of her early years. Once, when she was young, she inadvertently opened the front door to someone who had knocked and was then scolded so much by Ammamma for exposing herself to the outside world that she cried for three days afterwards.

When Bucchi was about fourteen years old, Ammamma's cousin, a Sreerangam nearing the end of his life, asked Ammamma to come and see him. He was a teacher on a small pension but with five children, who lived at his ancestral home in Gajapathinagaram in the neighbouring state of Andhra Pradesh. This was some 150 miles away from Ammamma's family home in Berhampur. However, known family members who shared the same caste operated an effective network, even before the advent of modern technology.

When Ammamma eventually arrived, the bedridden man boldly stated, 'You must allow my eldest son to marry Bucchi.' However much they may want to, a Hindu can't refuse the request of a dying person. This is for several reasons: respect for that person; the commonly held idea that people facing death speak words of truth or prophecy; but also fear that they could make your life miserable after death. (Fear so often reigns in Hinduism.) So Bucchi, at the age of fifteen, married his son, Shastri Sreerangam, who was to become my father.

Within one month of the wedding, the ailing man died. Very soon afterwards, Shastri found a job with the Indian Railways – one of the largest commercial employers in the world. He had to go wherever this job took him, all over the state of Orissa (an area similar to that of England and Wales combined, and now called Odisha). From his pay he had to support a widowed mother, two brothers, two sisters, a new wife and himself.

Bucchi, who had been used to being better off, looked forward to every opportunity to return to her mother's house with its comforts and comparative luxuries. In fact, because Shastri was frequently away with work, she made an excuse to go home for several days each month. Although it wasn't generally accepted for a married lady to go back to her own family very often, Bucchi felt she'd taken a step down by marrying Shastri with his lower earnings.

Nine months after her wedding, Bucchi gave birth to a baby. At long last, a grandchild for Ammamma! There was great joy on both sides of the family, not least because this baby was a boy. Many non-Hindus may wonder why a male child is so coveted. It's primarily because the birth of a boy (especially a firstborn) suggests to Hindus that the parents have done something good in their previous incarnation. Moreover, the birth of a boy guarantees the 'salvation' from hell of seven generations of grandparents, on both sides. In Hinduism, there is no particular judgement day and no permanent or eternal punishment (unless you include the endless cycles of reincarnation, which are hellish to an extent). Rather, hell is a place where someone is punished for the length of time deemed appropriate by Yama, the god of death, before Yama decides they can be reincarnated again. As nobody wants to face any of these hells, any means of escape is richly desired. The birth of a boy is like being granted a 'get out of hell free card'!

Another reason why a baby boy is especially desired is that he will continue the cherished family name, is likely to have a higher level of education, will earn more and, rather than costing dowry, will earn one when married. The significance given to a boy remains so entrenched in Indian society that it is little wonder that women start life from a disadvantaged position, through no fault of their own. (Thankfully, today such thinking is slowly starting to change in India.)

This baby boy thrived, bringing so much happiness and pride to the family – until he contracted smallpox. Though smallpox has now mercifully been eradicated, it was untreatable in those days and frequently fatal to infants in India. Nothing could be done for the little boy and, at just eighteen months old, he was defeated by the deadly virus.

Bucchi was heartbroken at the death of her firstborn son. This was compounded by the fact that Hinduism can make those already grieving feel worse rather than better. In Telugu, my family's language, smallpox is usually referred to as *ammavaru*, meaning 'the curse of a goddess'. This meant that in Bucchi's and the family's mind, the boy had actually died due to a curse by a goddess. So for decades afterwards until her death, Bucchi would search her soul to see what she may have done wrong to have caused this to happen. Rather than comforting her, the family pointed the finger instead, further deepening the grief and disgrace she bore.

Brahmin

Yet shortly after the death of her first child, Bucchi became pregnant again. Her brother-in-law, Surya – the religious fanatic and also a frequent visitor – suggested that everything possible should be done to bless this second pregnancy and avoid the outcome of the first. He fervently and unashamedly asked the gods for a child that would be very religious, live long and, above all, be male.

One of the ways they wanted to ensure this religiosity was by Bucchi hearing Hindu scriptures during her entire pregnancy. Surya was all too willing to read these every day. It's hard to see how he managed to find the time to actually do this, given the extent of all his own pious practices, but he did so nevertheless. In Hinduism there are a multitude of scriptures that tell different *puranas* (stories). One of the best-known, which Surya recited every afternoon throughout Bucchi's pregnancy, is *Bhagavata Purana*, the story of Vishnu, one of the three main gods of Hinduism. (The other two are Brahma, the creator, and Shiva, the destroyer). Central to it is Prahlad, a young boy whose actions increased religious devotion to Vishnu.[3]

Everything else humanly possible was done – such as visiting temples and seemingly endless reading of scriptures – so that this baby would be a devoutly religious male who would have a long life. Meanwhile, Bucchi's secret desire was that the child would be well educated and become a doctor. It's still extremely common in India for parents to want their child to join one of two professions: engineering or medicine.

Finally, early in the morning of Sunday 20 July 1947, I was born. There was great excitement in the house in Berhampur.

On the twelfth day of my life, as was the custom, a Hindu naming ceremony took place. As my dad was away at work – something I became used to – it was my mum's closest brother, my Uncle Krishna, who held me in his lap for the ceremony. Relatives – including my grandmother, Ammamma – showered their blessings on me, while marking my face with sacred ash in the hope that all the evil would be warded off from me. It's common for Hindus to name their children after gods and goddesses. As there are so many of them, there's plenty of choice! I was given the name Bhaskar, which means 'sun', something Hindus worship.

The joy experienced by my mum on having a baby boy was matched by the sorrow felt by my oldest aunt, Venkamma – or Akka as I'd call her. She continued to live in the miserable knowledge that she would never have the opportunity to become a mother. Yet longing for someone to love and care for, Akka asked my mum whether she could become my 'foster' mother, or godmother, to which my mum readily agreed. Even nowadays, it is common for an Indian child to have uncles or aunts (often without children of their own) taking on the role of parents in many practical matters.

When I was about three months old, I was entrusted to Akka. This was the beginning of a close and loving relationship, which has always been dear to me. Akka did everything expected of a mother: washing me, feeding me, telling me stories, introducing me to religious ceremonies and teaching me about the Hindu gods and goddesses. I became so attached to Akka in my early years that I didn't want to go to anyone else, including my own mum. Rather than being upset about this apparent rejection, though, my mum was relatively happy because it meant she was freed up to do other things. As I grew, my connection with Akka strengthened, based on mutual affection.

This loving relationship wasn't without some difficulties, however. Akka always had to make sure that she, a child widow, wasn't the first person I looked at in the morning, as that might bring a curse on me. Therefore, Akka would tell me to keep my eyes closed when I woke up until the photo of a god had first been placed in front of me. Or she'd gently direct me, with my eyes closed, to the home shrine, where we kept pictures and figures of idols. Only when I'd seen a god on opening my eyes, would she then allow me to look at her.

Akka did all this as a labour of love. Superstitions reign in Hinduism, controlling not only your personal behaviour but also your closest relationships. Meanwhile, continuous *puja* was made in the hope that the gods would be gracious to me. Years later, those requests were mercifully answered, but not in any way that my family could have anticipated.

2

A CONTENTED CHILDHOOD

When I was a few months old, Uncle Krishna gained entry into medical college. According to my family, my birth seemed to have opened the door for him to become a doctor, the cherished profession of India. At the same time, plans were being made for Uncle Krishna to get married.

But I was always the centre of attention, receiving hero status simply by being born a boy! As I grew, I was adored by my relatives. Being so loved, I must have been the most spoilt child on the street. All the utensils I had were made of silver. No common aluminium or stainless steel for me. I guess you could say I was born with a silver spoon in my mouth.

From the moment I was born, I was also repeatedly told by my relatives, and by Ammamma and Akka in particular, that I was one of the most fortunate children ever to have come into this world. Firstly, I was a human being; secondly, I was a boy; and thirdly, I'd been born into the priestly Brahmin caste – and so, undoubtedly, must have done plenty of good works, or *punya*, in my previous lives.

As many people know, this *punarjanna* (reincarnation) is one of the main beliefs in Hinduism. It guides a Hindu's every motive and action. In their thinking, a soul begins its journey as an inanimate object, such as a stone. Subsequently, it becomes a living being, starting in the plant kingdom and hopefully eventually gaining access into the animal kingdom. Then, as the *punya* increases with birth after birth, the soul begins its journey through the cycle of human beings, firstly being born into the lowest caste, the Sudra. By religious acts, good works, pilgrimages and so on, a person can increase their balance of goodness, or good karma, to climb the caste ladder, eventually reaching the coveted Brahmin (priestly) caste. However, if at any point during the cycle of incarnations the bad karma outweighs the good, it is likely that the soul will have to start part of the cycle all over again, perhaps going back to being a lower caste Sudra. Once you have attained a particular level, you have no guarantee that you won't go back down lower again in a future incarnation. For example, though I am a human now and think I am performing enough good works to attain a better incarnation next time, I may still be reincarnated as an animal or even a stone if my *punya* wasn't as good as I thought it was. It is like a cosmic game of snakes and ladders; until you reach the very end, you are never 'safe'.

In the 'normal' process, this cycle is considered to be 8,400,000 births long! Yes, that is nearly eight and a half million times of being born before the soul is released from the cycle and graduates into the final redemption called *moksha* (release). The ultimate hope of a Hindu is to be absorbed into the universe of Brahman, the 'supreme reality'. The concept of Brahman in Hinduism (not to be confused with my caste, Brahmin) represents the highest principle of a cosmic, formless, genderless, all-knowing, eternal reality in the universe, which is the cause of all things and unifies all things. The numberless cycles of reincarnation finally culminate in the Hindu reaching a state of release and utter bliss linked to Brahman.

I was therefore told that I was fortunate I wasn't an animal, a girl or a servant. However, I was also instructed that I needed to continue, as far as possible, to be a good boy in order to improve the chances of an even better next birth. Thus, my early years were punctuated by repeated affirmations of my already elevated status and a constant effort on my part to be as virtuous as I could be. All of this nurtured a deep sense of self-pride. I was unashamedly spoilt and, unsurprisingly, remember my early years as happy days.

Religious rituals

Once I could read for myself, one story fascinated me more than the scores of others: the story of Prahlad. At that time, I didn't realise it had been read to me in the womb. I'd want to read it or hear it at every possible opportunity.

If ever I was asked what I'd like to be when I grew up, I always replied that I wanted to be like Prahlad: someone who would be devoted to the god Vishnu.

Our ancestral home in Berhampur was situated on a street with several temples, or *mandirs*. At one end was the temple of a goddess known as Amma Waru, literally 'mother goddess'. She is famed in Berhampur, widely respected and worshipped as the local goddess. At the other end of the street was another temple dedicated to Jagannath, the god of Puri, a city in Orissa. Jagannath is known for demanding that his followers hurl themselves in front of a cart bearing his image, from which we get the anglicised word 'juggernaut'. A hundred metres or so from that was a temple of Kanyaka Parmasewari, a virgin goddess and one of the incarnations of the god Shiva's wife. There are believed to be 33 million gods in Hinduism (or 330 million, depending on your source), so you can imagine how many temples there must be. In short, my home city was besieged by Hindu temples.

Every year, the temple of Jagannath had a festival known as the Car (or Chariot) Festival. It's a popular one in the state of Orissa and was attended by my mum and uncle, who were committed devotees of Jagannath. It's common for most families to have a 'favourite' or 'local' god who they choose to worship most frequently. For example, Hindus in Calcutta (now called Kolkata) primarily worship the goddess Kali, while Bombay (Mumbai) Hindus predominantly worship the elephant god Ganesh.

Not only was our house surrounded by temples where I could worship, but I was also encouraged to worship at home. *Puja* (worship) is a ceremonial practice which may include offering incense, flowers and fruit (especially coconut and banana), as well as presenting various postures – for example, folding your hands, bowing down, full prostration on the floor or simply walking round in circles inside the room. I was also encouraged at home to perform *bhajan* (chanting a god's name) and read the scriptures. In short, there was no limit to the opportunities I had available to demonstrate my devotion to the gods, whether I was at home or out and about.

As with other religions, Hinduism has a common core of broad, universal tenets practised by the vast majority of Hindus worldwide. These include *puja* to idols, an emphasis on good works and abstinence from certain foods such as beef. However, it is worth noting that each locality or family may promote or prioritise particular religious practices based on their own traditions. My family was no exception.

Whenever I was afraid, I was taught to recite a short hymn in praise of one of two gods. The first was Hanuman, the monkey god. The second was Shiva, another of the three main gods, who's also called the king of demons. It seems strange, though, to pray to a demon when you are afraid.

Born into a priestly family and living in such a devout and intense religious atmosphere, I wasn't allowed to mix with any children from lower castes. At the time, I didn't question this, and it certainly didn't bother me. Apart from anything else, I was so utterly spoilt at home that I had nothing to be disappointed about.

I attended a Brahmin-only school, but had to take a spare set of clothes with me to school. This was because I mingled with children from other Brahmin sub-castes at school. Even though my classmates were Brahmins, I was from the prestigious Bharadwaja sub-caste – one of the highest divisions. My school wear became 'contaminated' by my classmates and I couldn't bring it into my house at the end of the day. I would first have to change into my 'uncontaminated' set of clothes to avoid defiling our home.

As you've no doubt already realised, I didn't have what most people would call a 'normal' childhood. I wasn't allowed to go and meet just anybody or play with other children as most evenings we would have some function which involved meeting religious people. Looking back on this now, I have mixed feelings. Sometimes, I feel sad that I had such a sheltered and narrow childhood, devoid of the usual innocent activities of playing with toys or making friends. At other times, I'm overwhelmed by God's goodness in reaching out to me in this void. At no time did I question my elders, who I know were doing what they thought was best. Even now, my sister Bharathi and I comment on how grateful we are for our upbringing.

I also still have happy memories of long evenings spent with Uncle Krishna and the woman he married. She had an amazing voice and went on to become a professional singer. We had a game where we'd listen to religious music on the radio, trying to be the first to guess which song it was. On the occasions when they were too busy to join with me, I'd simply chant god's name on my own until dinner time, and then go to bed.

I thus grew up secluded and sheltered, knowing little of the outside world. My daily life consisted of the following:

- a morning bath, which also made me ceremonially clean

- a brief time of worship at the household shrine

- breakfast, which was invariably leftover rice, served to me by my hard-working Akka

- going to school for the morning session, where I was a well-behaved and engaged student

- coming home for lunch, served by my ever-loving Akka (but only after I'd put on my second set of non-contaminated clothes)

- going back to school for the afternoon session (having put the contaminated clothes back on)

- returning home again (having once more changed out of the polluted clothes)

- having a snack provided by my all-caring Akka

- doing the obligatory homework

- spending the majority of the evening undertaking my religious studies, reading the scriptures aloud to my aunties and singing worship songs together.

Household shrines – a designated place for the household deities – are an important part of Hindu homes, though the size and grandeur will depend on the family's wealth and available space. The shrine is considered to be sacred and therefore is respected and revered, be it large or small. In my home, our shrine occupied the corner of one of our living rooms, which also doubled as the bedroom at night. When sleeping there, we therefore had to take care not to lie down with our feet pointing towards the corner where the shrine was situated, as this would have offended the gods.

The household deities or idols kept in the shrine differ from family to family according to their preferences and resources. We used to have five or six pictures of gods and goddesses on the wall. Below this was a wooden table, painted yellow with turmeric paste and with marks of red sacred ash around its border. On it stood three tiny, sofa-shaped, brass podiums on which we kept the icons, or small statues, of the gods. These were Shivalinga, which represented Shiva; a baby Krishna, an incarnation of the god Vishnu, in a crawling position; and also a small cone made of turmeric paste which signified Ganesh, the elephant-headed god, who is revered as the remover of obstacles. Our shrine also contained additional items to use in worship, such as sacred ash, incense sticks and brass oil-lamp burners. (In some homes, the oil is poured and a wick is placed in the oil so that the light burns all through the day and sometimes even in the night. No one is allowed to blow the light out, as this would be considered a bad omen.)

We were encouraged to look at a shrine – or a photo of a god that could be elsewhere in the house – the moment we opened our eyes in the morning. It was considered to be a great blessing to begin (and end) the day by doing so. My first and foremost deity was Saraswati, the goddess of learning, because she was considered to bestow educational success on her devotees, something I increasingly craved as a growing schoolboy. However, there is no set time or length for this worship, and no prescribed patterns, words or rituals. Each person can do it according to their own schedule and intentions. Having said that, in my family's practice, a married woman – after she has washed – must worship at the shrine while still wearing her wet clothes. Also someone must distribute *arati* (the sacred flame) and *prasad* (gifts that have been offered to the idols, typically a small, dairy-based sweet) to as many members of the household as possible. In some homes, it's the head of the household who should do this, but in my house this was always done by the married women, such as my uncle's wife or my mum. Widows, like my Akka, are never allowed near to a family's shrine because they are considered to be cursed, only being permitted to take part in worship rituals from a distance.

Another aspect of our family's religion was that each day of the week had its own particular deity. Mondays were predominantly for worshipping Shiva, either at home or in his temple. Tuesdays were dedicated to 'mother goddess'. For some reason, we didn't have a particular god for Wednesdays. Thursdays were often given over to the worship of the household deities, in particular Lakshmi, the goddess of wealth. On Fridays, we went to the temple of Jagannath. Saturdays were reserved for Lord Venkateswara. Then Sundays were largely given over to religious singing or watching religious Hindu films at the cinema. Many orthodox families devise their own programme of worship in this way.

Though to some readers this lifestyle may appear boring, I was actually happy and content. In fact, we never lacked excitement at home because we used to have celebrations for every possible occasion. With birthdays, death anniversaries and the festivals of various Hindu gods and goddesses, festivities were never far apart. All these also gave me the opportunity to interact with different people.

Of the umpteen celebrations and anniversaries, one of the most important is the death anniversary. In Hindu custom, remembering the anniversary of a relative's passing brings to the fore what happens in the afterlife. People do whatever they are able to ease their deceased relative's situation. For example, they may invite a priest round and feed him lots of food because the life of the departed soul depends partly on the contentment of the priest. They may even prepare food for the departed soul and leave it in a particular spot, waiting to see what happens to it. That would somehow, in their minds, indicate the present state of the departed one.

This particular emphasis on life after death and the need to satisfy the departed soul with food and *puja* highlighted two of my family's beliefs. Firstly, they believed that the departed soul was interested in and was reliant on what could be done to help them. The corollary of this is that, secondly, my family believed that those who remain should do what they can to improve someone's situation after they have died. Sometimes, my relatives would even give *daan* (gifts) on behalf of the departed person so that they could have a better life in the next incarnation. Through this I began to appreciate the reality and significance of death and the afterlife – albeit within the framework of Hinduism.

One of the things I'd been taught as a young child, including by spending time with my beloved Akka, was the recitation of Hindu scriptures and particularly the art of Hindu meditation. I spent hours and hours in worship in the form of yoga and in a concentrated effort of devoting my attention to Vishnu.

Many people know yoga only as a popular form of physical exercise but it is a Sanskrit (ancient Indian) word primarily meaning 'union' or 'absorption'. Yoga therefore denotes reaching a place of union with or absorption into someone or something. In Hinduism, this is seen as the soul's journey to find its meaning and purpose, and to enter into a state of unified consciousness. The *Bhagavad Gita*, perhaps the most important Hindu scripture, teaches that there are three ways for yoga to achieve the soul's desired end: the Way of Knowledge (Jnana Yoga), the Way of Devotion (Bhakti Yoga) and the Way of Duty (Karma Yoga). Yoga is therefore an inherently spiritual act – not just a few physical exercises.

As I was growing up, I wanted to follow the path of devotion in order to accrue good *moksha*, while my dad followed the path of duty. The yoga I performed therefore included chanting, meditation and worship.

Even my own family viewed me as eccentric because at times I'd spend hours oblivious to everything around me. Though most Hindus are content with going to a temple and paying the priest to chant on their behalf, I became an expert in chanting the 108 special names of Vishnu myself and then his full 1001 names. The number 108 holds particular significance in certain Hindu practices. Vishnu's 108 special names are considered sacred and it was firmly ingrained in me that repeated chanting of these 108 names would grant me additional blessing. Or I'd chant one individual name repeatedly for many hours. The example of Prahlad also gave me the impression that I could become like him if I persevered in spending long periods of time meditating and chanting.

Such was my childhood: chanting daily and meditating at home, visiting countless temples and celebrating festivals throughout the year. Not surprisingly, these experiences made an immense impression upon my young and fertile mind. I was happy, but blissfully ignorant. Perhaps only if something disturbing occurred would I question this status quo.

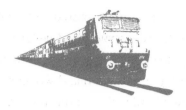

3

SATISFACTION FOLLOWED BY DISILLUSIONMENT

As my dad worked for Indian Railways, we could travel on the whole network free of charge. I couldn't even begin to write about all the temples we were able to visit due to this perk of the job. One memorable excursion, though, when I was twelve, was to a prominent pilgrimage centre in India: Tirumala temple in Tirupati, in the state of Andhra Pradesh. My sister Bharathi, who was ten, also came. (Although by this time I had three brothers and two sisters, I only remember us two oldest children going on pilgrimages.)

Tirupati – like Rome – is situated on seven hills, and its temple is on top of one of those hills – perhaps like the Temple of Jupiter on ancient Rome's Capitoline

Hill. Millions of Hindus go there every year to worship a god known as Venkateswara or Balaji. He is one of the 'unorthodox' (that is, outside of the ten main) but popular incarnations of Vishnu, and is widely accepted and honoured.

The first part of our journey was to Renigunta, which took eighteen hours, a standard duration for Indian train journeys, such is the vast size of my sub-continent. This fact, combined with the average speed of the Indian rolling stock, means you will frequently hear people exclaim that they can walk quicker than the train travels. We stayed overnight in a charity hostel, provided for visitors to the temple.

The next morning, my family and I boarded a bus which was full of fellow pilgrims. There was a sense of expectation and a recognition of the privilege of visiting a much-loved temple. People therefore didn't dwell on the discomfort or inconvenience of the journey, and so it passed by peaceably. Following a winding and precarious ride of about five hours (a short one by Indian standards), my parents, Bharathi and I finally arrived.

The temple doors opened at seven in the morning, but pilgrims would start queuing long before then. So at 4.30 a.m., when we joined the line of people, it was already over a mile long. (Even then India was a nation of half a billion people.) While people were waiting, regular, rhythmic chanting could be heard in unison. This was in Telugu, not only my family's language but also the main language of our state: '*Edu Kondala Vada! Edu Kondala Vada!*' ('The one who lives on seven hills! The one who lives on seven hills!'). This chanting went on for hours – which, for most of the pilgrims gathered there, was nothing compared to the days and weeks of chanting to which they were accustomed. I heartily joined in along with my family.

There are over two thousand steps from the bottom of the hill to the temple at the top. Many pilgrims choose to climb them as they believe that's more meritorious than being driven up, but we took the bus to the top as even in those days my mum would have struggled with the climb. It is because this pilgrimage is physically and mentally demanding – especially due to the sheer length of travelling and waiting in large crowds – that many Hindus don't bring their children to Tirupati; those who do typically leave their children in the hostel. So Bharathi and I were privileged to actually go up to the temple with our parents.

There, thousands of people waited expectantly and confidently that Balaji would accept their *puja* – after all, they were there at great personal cost. Then again, this god was also feared because he had a reputation for exacting penalties if pilgrims didn't fulfil pledges they'd made. Once worshippers finally left the mountain, it was usually with a sense of relief that they'd survived the event unscathed. Today, the visitor website reassures pilgrims that 'constant patrol by security forces [is provided] to prevent pilgrims from being cheated or robbed by unscrupulous elements', so I wonder whether this has made any difference to the attitude of giving now.

Balaji is known as a god who likes human hair offered by his devotees. Consequently, the temple is full of barbers, ready to shave the heads of willing worshippers in exchange for a fee. Millions of babies have also been taken there by their parents for the prestigious shaving off of their birth hair, or *mundan,* which – as in many cultures and religions – is a widespread and popular custom. One explanation for this is that many Hindus believe birth hair carries remnants of bad karma from the previous life. Incidentally, as barbers are ceremonially unclean, anyone who's had their hair cut must then undertake a prescribed ceremonial bath.

To return to my visit, eventually the temple doors opened and the queue slowly progressed. My family and I would be able to glance at the granite idol for a grand total of five seconds. But my dad hadn't undertaken that arduous journey to look at the statue for such a measly length of time. Rather, he paid a significant sum of money, equivalent to one week's wages, to buy us a private viewing of the idol, where we could worship it for sixty seconds. It's noteworthy, though perhaps unsurprising, that this god may be richer than the Indian government. In those days, that temple alone took some 400,000 rupees (approximately £5,000) a day, and some sources say that today it takes in 10 billion rupees a year (approximately £115 million). We were certain that it was well worth the expense and the effort, even though it bought us only one minute with our idol.

Thus, after hours of travel, waiting and chanting, my dad and I, accompanied by my mum and Bharathi, stared at the sights before us. The priest placed drops of sacred water, from the copper vessel in front of the idol, into our palms. We ingested it, feeling self-righteous, and returned home, satisfied that we had accomplished a pilgrimage to this glorious temple. For me, this was a significant childhood event: I'd undertaken something very holy and notable that many people older than me wouldn't manage to do in their whole lifetime.

We wanted to maximise our opportunities on this round trip, and so we also stopped at a second temple and then a third, at Annavaram, about eighty miles in the direction of home. Annavaram has a temple dedicated to Satya Narayana, which is one of the special 108 names for Vishnu. For some reason, Hindus like to approach and worship their gods under different incarnations or names. The name Satya – the Sanskrit word for 'truth' – was added to underline to devotees that Narayana is truthful. The fact that he's in a place called Annavaram, meaning 'get what you ask for', reinforces the idea that answers are guaranteed. People therefore flock to this temple, hoping that their requests will be met. This, combined with the fact it's a well-respected site, means that hundreds of thousands of Hindus visit the Satya Narayana temple each month.

The four of us went inside the shrine with an offering prepared in advance by my dad. He passed the offering plate to the priest in his enclosure, asking him to conduct the worship on our behalf. The priest duly took it, asking for my father's and grandfather's names, along with the name of the sub-caste to which my family belonged. My dad told the priest that we were Gotra Brahmins and specifically Bharadwajas. The moment the priest heard the prestigious name Bharadwaja, he hastily put the offering aside, hurried out of the enclosure, threw himself at my dad's feet and began to worship him, a fellow human being. As you can imagine, my dad was quite taken aback.

The priest explained, 'I have no authority to conduct worship on your behalf because your sub-caste and that of the god you have come to worship are the same. My sub-caste is lower than yours, so you are almost equal to god. How can I conduct worship or bless you when you are superior to me and almost equal to the god that is being worshipped here?'

This incident remains fresh in my mind even to this day. Now I had discovered what type of priestly family I'd been destined to join. I realised that I'd been born into a family whose sub-caste was equal to that of a god, and that even a respected priest would worship us.

Disappointing doctrine

Up to this point, I hadn't questioned my upbringing or my religion. But when four unexpected and disturbing events took place, they shook the foundations of my being and changed the trajectory of my life.

The first event was the death of my grandmother, Ammamma. I clearly remember coming back from school one afternoon when a lady passing by told me indifferently that my grandmother had died that morning. So much for breaking bad news. Strangely, I wasn't adversely affected by her death straight away. She had endured painful stomach cancer for many years (which seemed an injustice since she had been a staunch vegetarian and teetotaller). She'd struggled for months, having to go to the hospital in Cuttack, a five-hour train journey away, to receive the unpleasant treatment known to us as cobalt therapy. So initially, I saw her death as relief from her terrible pain and suffering. I was also glad that she could look forward to a better incarnation – given her forbearance and cheerfulness through all she'd suffered in this life, I was sure she would have accrued good karma.

But I did become affected by her death when twelve days later, and then for thirty consecutive days, a priest from the local temple came to our house each afternoon to read *Garuda Purana*. This religious scripture has thirty chapters describing the soul's journey after physical life. As its name, 'Book of the Eagle', suggests, the soul soars up like an eagle for a long time before reaching its final destination: either coming back in a reincarnated form or ending up in one of the hells, suffering and paying penance for all its misdeeds during past incarnations.

I found the book fascinating with all its punishment, pain, suffering and agony, and its suggestions of how those left on earth could help the departed relative's pains and problems through sacrifices, offerings and gifts. One day, as the priest was reading these scriptures, I told him I had a question: 'Do you have assurance that you will go to the Supreme Reality, Brahman, when you die?'

Disappointingly, he replied, 'No, I don't.' He tried to appease me, however, with a story. In the hearing of everyone present, he dogmatically announced, 'Twenty-three incarnations ago, I approached Shiva in his abode called Kailash and I asked him how much merit I had. He said to me, "You have 69 per cent merit; when you complete 100 per cent, then you will get release." So for the last twenty-three incarnations, I've been trying my best to achieve that 100 per cent and I haven't managed it yet. I don't know now if I still have 69 per cent or less, and I don't know how much longer I need to struggle to obtain more.'

I looked him straight in the eye and exclaimed, unabashed, 'You mean to say that in the last twenty-three incarnations you haven't been able to complete the remaining 31 per cent of meritorious acts?'

To this he simply replied, 'No.'

'But you're a priest?'

'Yes, I am.'

'And you worship the gods all the time?'

'Yes, I do.'

'You help others to worship the gods?'

'Yes, of course.'

'Yet your merit is not complete. Do you know how many more incarnations you need?'

'No, son – it may be hundreds, but it may be thousands.'

To hear from such a religious person that twenty-three lives couldn't help him to make any improvement in his karma was a shattering blow to my young spirit. So I asked him, 'Is it no good, then, becoming an officiating priest and working in the temple twenty-four hours a day?'

'No, son. It's no good at all. In the story of Rama you are taught that anyone who works as a priest in the present life often comes back in the form of a dog in the next incarnation.'

I knew exactly which story, or *purana*, he was referring to: the *Ramayana Purana*. In this tale, King Rama is presented with a case where a dog asks for justice for being hit by a passer-by in an unprovoked attack. When Rama is about to punish the passer-by, the dog requests to be allowed to make a suggestion: 'Instead of punishing him with lashes or fines, why not instead make him a priest in a temple?' Rama is surprised by this curious request and wants to understand the reason for it. The dog elaborates, 'I was a priest in my previous incarnation and, because I stole from god, I've been punished by being born as a dog. I want him to know what it's like to be a dog.'

The implication that priests steal is never lost on anyone. This story also implies that being an officiating priest in the temple doesn't mean that you'd be released from reincarnation cycles. Rather, it means that you could earn the punishment of returning as a dog in the next life. Dogs are simultaneously despised (as common vermin, who carry disease) and revered (as embodying former priests) by Hindus in India.

This priest's revelation was devastating to me. My young mind was starting to find that no amount of religion, good works or sincerity would constitute any help in avoiding hell. It was a disturbing recognition that there didn't seem to be any escape from the prospects of either going to hell or coming back in yet another form of lower life.

After this first key event, I became obsessed with meeting more religious people. I divided the world into two categories: those who knew they had *moksha* and those who didn't. If I could find anyone in the first category, my motive would be to find out from them how I could achieve *moksha*, obtaining salvation from the endless cycles of reincarnation.

Is this how it all ends?

The second devastating event involved Ammamma's younger brother, Yagna Narayana.

Before the British colonised India, the sizable country was made up of small kingdoms, ruled over by locally appointed kings, or *rajas*. Yagna Narayana was the finance minister to the then king of the state of Orissa, in Jeypore. Wealthy and influential, he was highly respected in the family. More than that, Yagna Narayana was able to not only read but also recite in Sanskrit the *Vedas*, which educated Hindus consider to be the most important or authoritative scriptures. Although it's permissible for Hindus to access the scriptures in their own local language, it's more meritorious to know them in the original language, Sanskrit.

Yagna Narayana used to worship his gods every day for at least two hours. When visiting him, I was fascinated to see the little idols that he kept. These were small, stone replicas of the larger idols in the temples. He would keep them in a closed box until after his morning ceremonial bath. Then he would open the box and sit on the floor in a cross-legged position, chanting and anointing the idols with milk and oil.

I observed this practice so intently that I memorised everything he did, until eventually I too was able to recite parts of the *Vedas* in Sanskrit. As a result, I'd often be asked to officiate at religious ceremonies, delivering them with such gusto that people would applaud me. They were impressed at my ability to know the scriptures in their original language with the correct diction and intonation, with enthusiasm and confidence, and at a relatively young age.

Yagna Narayana and I enjoyed each other's company and became inseparable. I'd call him Bojja Tata. ('Bojja' means 'stomach' and 'Tata' means 'grandfather'. He had a generously proportioned stomach, hence the nickname.) I may not have had any friends of my own age because of my isolated childhood, but with the affection and company of Bojja Tata, I wasn't bothered.

As with all religions, Hinduism is expressed through various sects. The two main sects are the Vaishnavites and the Shivites. The Vaishnavites primarily follow Vishnu and can be easily identified by the marking on their forehead: a U shape with an extra line down its centre, applied by paint or sacred ash. The Shivites primarily worship Shiva and are readily identified by three horizontal painted or ash lines across their forehead. Bojja Tata was a Shivite, and would frequently tell me that Shiva was the most accessible of all the gods because he would willingly answer any questions posed to him and grant any wish.

By now I was aged fourteen, and questions about life and death had been growing within me. Not least I wanted to know how I could get to Brahman, the 'supreme reality', and so avoid endless reincarnation cycles. I thought that if anyone could provide the answer, it would be my devout Bojja Tata. Seldom had there been a more pious Hindu, as far as I was concerned. Bojja Tata's answers to my enquiries were usually given in the form of a *purana*, always ending with Shiva being the answer to all my questions. I thought, therefore, that the best thing I could do was to hold on to Shiva until he told me how I could get to him when I died.[4]

At some point I came to discover that for all Bojja Tata's devotion, knowledge, worship, incantations and ceremonial washings, this fervent Hindu Brahmin was nevertheless afraid of dying. He would often concede that the future was unknown and admit that he had no confidence about what lay ahead. Though this was yet another blow to me, at least he was honest.

Inevitably, in due course, the day came for him to leave this earth. At seventy-five, he was racked by age and ill health, and death approached. But in the final moments of his life, something horrifying happened. Despite the fact he was a physical giant, my great-uncle began to weep like a child. The man I'd admired and respected now alarmed me as he shook uncontrollably. He pleaded, unintelligibly, in loud desperation. But none of us could understand what was wrong. His wife and children tried to console him, but to no avail.

'What's the matter? Why are you so restless?'

'In front of me I see the angels of the god of death, Yama!' he screamed.

With chilling detail, Bojja Tata then tried to describe what he saw. To him it had appeared as real as any of us standing in the room. He told us of two dark figures of horrifying appearance with horns on either side of their head. With malicious and mocking laughter, they were tormenting him: 'Come! Your time is up. We have come to escort you to hell.'

Bojja Tata was terrified of them and tearfully pleaded for more time. It was immensely painful to see the desperate state of this man screaming in inconsolable anguish. Despite his frenzied pleading, it seems the demons would not yield. With agony, seeing his destiny was hell, my great-uncle breathed his last.

Witnessing this shook me to my core. I can hardly describe its impact. Not only had I lost a dearly loved one, but it opened up a bewildering reality to me. How could such a devout man die like this? Why would Shiva willingly save the life of Markandeya, a sixteen-year-old boy (as recounted in the *Markandeya Purana*), and yet not save Bojja Tata, who'd spent a long lifetime faithfully worshipping him and accruing good karma in his name? Despite all my great-uncle's religious devotion and practice, knowledge and understanding, earnest and sincere *puja*, it all seemed to have come to nothing. Decades of religious fervour, observance and sacrifice were for what? To me, Bojja Tata apparently ended up in hell, knowing the consequences full well.

I was troubled by the thought that if my devoted great-uncle could face such a horrific death – being summoned even by demons – how could anyone ever hope to be free of hell and reincarnations? How on earth could I stop this cycle of life and death ad infinitum? How could I escape the fearful clutches of the angels of death carrying me away to face the horrors of hell when my time came? There must be another way, some means by which I could bypass the countless reincarnation cycles and attain ultimate release – whatever that might mean.

For months afterwards, I felt like a pilgrim in a barren land. I had been devoted to so much religious toil, but for so little gain, if Bojja Tata's last moments were anything to go by. Clearly I'd have to perform abundantly more good works than he had performed if I was to attain the *moksha* I was so desperate to have. This problem was to become my preoccupation and obsession for the next five years. The third distressing event further magnified this fixation.

The pressures of family life

In the meantime, I completed my high-school exams in March 1963, the end of the academic year. During the six-week holiday that followed, my Uncle Suryam taught me that all-important skill invaluable throughout India – how to ride a bike. Then, in May 1963, at the age of fifteen, I began my pre-university (Pre-U) course at the local Khallikote College in Berhampur. My dad graciously gave me a Humber bike so that I could get myself from my Uncle Krishna's house, where I'd be living, to my college. As was typical in India, I called this prestigious uncle 'Doctor Uncle'. In fact, it was (and largely still is) seen as disrespectful to name an older relative with their name – they were only ever referred to by their title or relationship.

The Pre-U course was similar to taking A levels but lasted only one year. The four subjects I took were maths, physics, chemistry and biology. Since my early childhood, I had excelled at and adored numbers, so I worked hard and with enthusiasm at the first three (often called 'MPC' by Indian students). My mum had simultaneously spent my whole childhood telling me to become a doctor. But given my absolute aversion to dissections and the utter repulsion I felt for anything in the biology classroom, there was no way I could ever fulfil my mum's wishes. (I wasn't even accustomed to cutting meat on a plate as we were strict vegetarians.) Neither did the stories my doctor uncle related of medical school and cutting up corpses do anything to help me change my mind. So I let my biology efforts lapse to the minimum, merely attending lessons and little more. Subsequently, though I did well at MPC, I failed the most crucial subject for a medical degree: biology. This automatically meant I wouldn't be able to study medicine.

This caused no small fracas at home. My mum and doctor uncle both wanted me to become a doctor in the same measure that I didn't want to become a doctor. My mum had so many hopes pinned on her eldest son becoming a doctor that it was difficult for her to accept the situation. I wanted to pursue engineering.

There was also family friction because everyone flocked to doctor uncle's home. Living there were not only him, his wife and their seven children (they had eleven eventually), but also myself and my sister Bharathi; my Uncle Joga and his family; and my Aunty Chinna Dodda and her family: four families under one roof. Not surprisingly, my aunt became disgruntled that so many people were living off her husband's precious earnings. Given these numerous family tensions, I avoided being in the house as much as possible.

For the first time in my life, I therefore started to make friends with people from lower castes – much to my family's disgust and shame. I'd also go to restaurants, coffee houses and the cinema, spending time with my wealthier counterparts doing worldly things. There is nothing wrong with these places per se, but my motivation was to idle my time away, avoiding family and home. I subconsciously took on a rebellious attitude towards my own flesh and blood. None of this made me feel any happier.

Now that I'd tasted independence and a degree of rebellion, and given that the medical door really was closed, I did what most young people opted for after their Pre-U: I joined a BSc course at the same local college. Unbeknown to my family (though I can't see how it would have come as a surprise to them), I enrolled myself for

MPC – and not for biology. I duly started the degree in May 1964. However, my heel-digging insolence as a teenager, combined with the fact that I wouldn't now be able to do a medical degree and the pressure cooker of their domestic life, became too much for my uncle and aunt. It all caused an irreparable rift. Therefore, though they'd provided for and accommodated me at their home for a long time, I was essentially thrown out.

I had to return to my dad's house in Bondamunda in Orissa. At the age of seventeen, where else could I go? I also had to abandon my BSc at Khallikote.

4

TURBULENT TEENAGE YEARS

The year of my birth, 1947, saw the Partition of India, in which British India was divided into two separate countries: India and Pakistan. The political tensions and social uprisings caused by this had resulted in the death of hundreds of thousands of people, and the injury and violation of many more. The following year fighting took place over the stunningly beautiful northern state of Kashmir, claimed by both India and Pakistan. It isn't called 'Partition' for nothing. Now in 1965, while I was into my teenage years, a second war with Pakistan was taking place over Kashmir.

At this time, I was still living with my mum and dad at home in Bondamunda, with all my brothers and sisters. There were six of us: me (who had turned eighteen); my sister Bharathi (sixteen); my brother Krishna (thirteen);

my brother Prasad (eleven); my younger sister, Prabha (nine); and lastly my youngest brother, Mohan (eight).

This was the backdrop to the third significant experience that galvanised my inner conflict and need to be guaranteed *moksha*.

Disappointing deity

Most citizens of war-wracked countries will attempt to carry on with life as normal, if this is at all possible. Nothing would stop my family's frequent attendance at religious pageants or get-togethers. These took the form of people gathering in a temple or in somebody's home to chant one particular sentence: *'Jai venkatesa srinivasa'* (meaning 'victory to god' and 'victory to the dweller with wealth'). We would chant the same sentence repeatedly for three hours non-stop in various tunes and forms.

During these times of incessant chanting, a spirit – which we interpreted as being a god – would come upon someone, who would thereby become possessed by it and fall. The others present needed first to make sure that the devotee was unconscious, so that they could be certain they were addressing a spirit. Therefore, strange though it may sound, they would put soap and camphor on to his or her palm and set light to it. The camphor burns but no pain is felt and no burn marks appear. Sometimes, the person would even swallow the burning camphor and seemingly nothing would happen to them. Once the unconsciousness of the person had been confirmed, the others would ask them (or rather, the spirit that was upon the person) important questions regarding problems or circumstances, such as marriage, jobs or sickness.

During one particular occasion, this happened to the mother of a high-flying engineer on the Indian Railways. My mum (who had decided to return to formal education and gain some basic qualifications) asked the spirit who possessed her, 'Will I pass my forthcoming matriculation exam?'

The reply was affirmative.

My mum wasn't satisfied so she boldly asked another question: 'It's eighteen years since I was a student, prior to becoming a mother. My mind is in no condition to study. How can I possibly pass?'

The spirit within the woman replied, 'I will go and take your exam for you and therefore you will pass.'

My mum was thrilled that the god was going to go with her and write her answers for her – what a great devotee she must be. However, not wishing to take any chances, she still studied hard and prepared as best she could.

The exams were completed, but when the results came a couple of months later, they were contrary to my mum's genuine expectations. She discovered she hadn't passed; she'd failed. That was a blow to her and to the family.

Although my family may not have paid much attention to the glaring contradiction, I certainly did. I clearly remembered that the spirit or god had said, 'I will go and take your exam for you and therefore you will pass.' Yet despite the god's promise, my mum had failed. It wasn't lost on me that the god's word hadn't come to pass.

Not only was my longing for answers further exacerbated by this third shock, but I was once more about to be thrown into turbulence by another death.

Sudden death

A few weeks later, just as spring 1965 was turning to summer, came a night I will never forget. I was sitting with my dad's younger brother, Surya Narayana Murty, or Chinna Nanna as we called him. Though technically my uncle, Chinna Nanna was only a couple of years older than me and therefore more like an older brother. We chatted until nearly midnight, and then I said to him, 'I'll go to bed now.' (It isn't an Indian custom to say goodnight.) Little did I realise that those would be the last words I ever spoke to my uncle: he didn't wake up the following morning.

This was obviously a devastating shock for everyone, particularly for me because I'd lost not just an uncle but a companion. How could someone so close to me in age die like that, with no warning whatsoever? We never did find out the cause of his sudden death. In a time when post-mortem examinations were rare and death certification standards poorly defined, many unexpected deaths were left unexplained. Additionally, a combination of hot weather and the demands of religious customs surrounding death meant that dead bodies were cremated as promptly as was practically possible.

In accordance with the Hindu custom, the older male members of the family, including my dad, and a few friends from the neighbourhood had the body cremated. Hinduism requires this to happen before sunset. My unkempt and sobbing dad, who had received the devastating news at work, some eight hours away, therefore had needed to hurry back, managing to get home just prior to the sunset deadline.

The dead body of my uncle was laid out on a bamboo stretcher on the ground outside my house. My relatives poured cups of water over it. They washed the body with their own hands. Then some fire was carried in a clay pot behind the funeral bier as it made its solemn way to the cremation ground. My uncle's body was laid to rest on the pyre, the pile of wood placed in the centre of the funeral ground. My dad transferred the flame on to the wood beneath my uncle's head. The flames resolutely performed their duty towards the wood and the flesh.

I wasn't allowed to attend any of the events involved in the cremation. Although I would have found the sights disturbing, the real reason for this was that my family feared me asking more questions. Had I observed all of these things, combined with the slow walk of the men returning after dusk to the hollow home, indeed I would have had many more questions.

After four days, my dad and others returned to the cremation ground to collect the ashes. I remember distinctly that the ashes were brought back to the house in an unassuming Ovaltine tin. But my only emotion was that of curiosity: why was it so important to retain the ashes? I was told, as has been mentioned before, that it is possible to help a departed soul even though they have died. As is so common in India, the family's mission was to transport my uncle's ashes hundreds of miles away to Hindu's most holy city: Varanasi (or Benares) in the north of India. There they would be faithfully immersed in the sacred River Ganges, also known to Indians as the goddess Ganga, which supposedly has the capacity to wash away the sins of the living and the dead.

Although it may sound disrespectful, I wasn't particularly concerned about my uncle's remains. However, when I found out that my dad, as the oldest male, would have the responsibility to take the ashes to Varanasi, I begged to go with him in order to worship the god Shiva in his special temple on the banks of the river. It would be a great privilege, especially for a young person. I had a one-track mind by now: anything that could provide an answer to my as yet unanswered question of how to attain *moksha* was worth any discomfort or inconvenience. So within a month or so – which was as soon as we were able – my dad, mum, sister Bharathi, the Ovaltine tin and I travelled the long, slow journey by train to Varanasi.

Pilgrimage of a lifetime

All four of us had mixed feelings about our trip: on the one hand, we felt full of sorrow for Chinna Nanna; and on the other, we were warmed with the excitement of seeing the sacred Ganges for the first time in our lives. This was especially so as countless Hindus never get to see the holy river at all, even in modern times.

Having travelled for the best part of twenty-four hours by train to Varansi, we were relieved to disembark. Varanasi was characteristically crowded then, as it is nowadays. We went to our hotel to sleep and wash. Then, the following morning – which couldn't come fast enough as far as I was concerned – we made our way expectantly down to the river bank.

Despite my impatience to get to the temple, I felt a sense of relief that we were helping my uncle. We were performing this ritual out of love for him, in the knowledge that through it we'd be increasing his merit and thereby helping his next incarnation. Furthermore, once we'd immersed ourselves in the river, our own karma would be elevated.

I was also pleased that we spoke Hindi – the language of Varanasi – as it made transactions easier, such as commandeering a priest to perform the ceremonies. Although the mother tongue of both my parents was Telugu, the language of Andhra Pradesh, my dad had learnt to speak Hindi because that's the lingua franca of the railways. To overcome the language barrier, many Hindus even bring their local priest with them – an expensive and cumbersome solution.

We finally reached the bank of the sacred Ganges. Millions of people have bathed there, set their hopes on its powers and scattered the ashes of loved ones there, and now so was I! (Incidentally, many others have sadly drowned there or been trampled to death at the unofficial *Kumbh Mela* festival.) We approached the water's edge at a particularly prestigious spot called *Dashashwamedh Ghat* (translated as 'ten horse sacrifice bank'). The symbolism of this *ghat* (bank) of the Ganges is that anything religious performed there takes on the equivalent value of a sacrifice of ten horses – where a horse is seen as the greatest sacrifice certain Hindus can make. My dad was wearing the necessary ceremonial dress – a white silk *dhoti* with a golden border that he'd brought with him especially. (A *dhoti* is a piece of cloth folded in a particular manner around the man's waist.) He then selected the most respectable-looking priest from the many who lingered at the water's edge hoping for some custom.

Having purchased a clay pot into which we carefully transferred my uncle's ashes, we solemnly carried it to the water's edge. We followed the priest into the Ganges and then we worshipped the sun, as is stipulated for any ceremony in the Ganges. To do this, you must first stand knee-deep in the water, facing the sun. Next, you bend down to scoop up some water in your hands, lift them up to the sun and then let the water pour down – as a kind of offering to the sun. This has to be repeated twice.

Hindu priests are always ready with their dramatic language at such times, and this is no exception. Everything possible is said and done so that the departed soul can have its sins completely washed away. Our hired priest scattered handfuls of my uncle's ashes on to the surface of the water. He then lit a tea light candle, releasing it on to the water. Into this wake he lastly threw some flowers. Everything floated away and we had thus successfully fulfilled our obligations.

While all this was occurring, I grasped the opportunity to question the priest – as had become my practice. I turned to him and asked, 'Sir, will my uncle live on?'

'Yes, he will.'

'But sir, will my uncle have a better life next time?'

'Yes, he will have a better life in the next incarnation because his sins have been washed away by the goddess Ganga.'

I was happy enough with this answer, especially as it was being given in the Ganges. Since many stories have been told about the efficacy of the holy river, and the longing of every Hindu to take a holy dip in it, I believed him implicitly – until I had reason shortly afterwards to question it.

No trip to any Indian city is ever complete without a visit to its temple – especially in Varanasi, the greatest Hindu city of them all. So we went to its Vishwanath temple, which is dedicated to Shiva. Each evening, a special ceremony takes place just prior to the closing of the doors for the night. This is to put the god to sleep, but is, paradoxically, a noisy affair, with brass gongs sounding, trumpets blaring, cymbals crashing and bells ringing. It's a deafening cacophony. (The fallacy of a god who needs to sleep occurred to me much later.)

Nevertheless, despite all the commotion, something happened to me and I fell into a trance, oblivious to everything else. I felt I was surrounded by the very presence of the god we were putting to sleep. I remember feeling enveloped by an unusual presence. Though I was lost to all that was happening around me for only a couple of minutes, the bliss I felt at the time is beyond words. The priest conducting the ceremony must have observed a look of radiant delight on my face because he stopped, approached my dad and commented, 'Sir, that boy of yours has such a glow. He has seen something today few people would ever see and he has been in the presence of god himself for the last few minutes. You are privileged to have such a son.'

I am still not able to explain adequately the nature or meaning of what happened there. However, the key thing is that despite these 'privileged' religious experiences, all I wanted was the reassurance of knowing how I could obtain relief from the terrifying cycle of reincarnation.

More religious experiences

On Saturdays, we usually held religious gatherings in our house, with members of the community regularly joining us. As I have already explained, during some chanting sessions someone would fall unconscious to the floor as they were possessed by a spirit. The others there would then address that person as god himself. Some months after going to Varanasi – while the men were at work – that happened to me. I obviously have no recollection of this at all, having been unconscious. However, my mum told me later that I'd been possessed by a spirit who apparently said that this possession would keep happening to me for six months.

All the ladies present became respectful towards me after that, but my mum was devastated. Religion, though important, certainly came a distant second in her life. She realised that the more religious I became, the less likely it would be that I'd ever become a doctor. Her fear was that the gods would demand me to be a priest. In the end, I tried to placate my mum by telling her that I'd first study wholeheartedly (although not medicine) and then work to support my younger brother Krishna through university. Only once I reached the age of about thirty would I renounce the world, become a priest and seek to deliver myself from any more reincarnations.

As I said, I had a one-track mind. My ever-regretful mum, recognising that she wouldn't be able to change my determined (or, as she might say, stubborn) mind, tacitly agreed with, or at least reluctantly relented, to this plan. And yet I wasn't satisfied, even though I spent hours and days in meditation, chanting the names of gods, and could have spirits dwelling in me. Even all this couldn't mollify me. I was still no nearer to discovering how to gain my coveted *moksha*.

The cow comes home

Six months after we returned from the River Ganges with the priest's assurance that my young uncle's next incarnation would be a good one, I was still perplexed. As my uncle had been a human being, a male and of the good Bharadwaja sub-caste of the prestigious Brahmin caste, I didn't understand how his next incarnation could actually be superior to the one he'd just had. I wondered whether this question had crossed any of my relatives' minds, but I would never ask them because that would have been disrespectful.

My young uncle's death was the backdrop to the fourth key event to shake my religious foundations. What happened soon afterwards would help to change the direction of my life, as surely as a points change diverts the route of a train.

Around that time, one of the cows we owned gave birth to a calf. Hindus usually respect cows, which are seen as sacred animals, by caring for them and even worshipping them. There are many social and religious reasons for the veneration of cows, but perhaps the most compelling is that Krishna, in one of his incarnations, was a cow-herder, or *gopal*. It seems that anything merely associated with a Hindu god also takes on religious or holy significance. However, we kept our calf outside in a shed because to keep them in the house would be totally impractical.

Within days of the new calf's birth, we tried to tether it, but had difficulty in doing so because he was unruly and utterly reluctant to be tied down. Even when we eventually succeeded, he struggled with all his might to break the rope. We were concerned that he might inadvertently strangle himself, which would only add to our sins, so we had no choice but to release him. He wandered here and there in his new-found freedom, but then had the audacity to walk right into our bungalow and head straight into the living room. He placed himself in a particular corner, sitting down quite purposefully on the floor. We were worried that he might damage the floor (especially as our home was provided by Indian Railways), so we drove him away. But within a few minutes, he came back again and sat in the same spot.

When this happened repeatedly, my mum's curiosity was aroused: 'Bhaskar, why is it that this calf wants to sit in that very spot?' The more she thought about it, she realised that every day when my late uncle used to return from his working day, he would sit in that exact spot to have his cup of tea and unwind. The calf would do nothing else but sit there quietly with his big, brown eyes, regarding us. Excited that the calf was possibly a reincarnation of my young uncle, my mum determined to find out the truth.

It may sound funny, but my mum approached the calf and asked it directly, 'Are you my brother-in-law?' Truly, the calf moved its head up and down in the form of a nod, apparently indicating that he'd understood the question and that he was indeed a reincarnation of my uncle. Not surprisingly, this was confirmation enough to my mum, who was greatly excited that my uncle had returned to the same house in the form of a cow.

However, the ensuing elation felt by the rest of my family at my 'uncle's' return was balanced in equal measure by my frustration. I was extremely disappointed, and even more perplexed, because I'd hoped that after all the prescribed Hindu requirements we'd followed for him, my uncle would have been guaranteed at least an equal incarnation. Moreover, the Varanasi priest's unequivocal promise was that my uncle would have an even better incarnation. How, by any stretch of the imagination, could this be the case if in reality he'd come back in the form of a calf, a speechless animal? Why did this paradox not seem to trouble or at least occur to anyone else in the family?

I was increasingly despondent and even more agitated. All our efforts for my uncle had come to absolutely nothing. There was no hope for my uncle and therefore no hope at all for me. What hope was there for anyone?

Calling up the dead

To add to my deeds of zeal, I'd learned the ability to call up supposedly dead spirits to find out information from them. One method of invoking spirits, commonly known around the world, is with an Ouija board. Gathering around an Ouija board was a common occurrence in my neighbourhood. Although my doctor uncle prohibited the activity taking place in his house, his wife would often engage in it in his absence, such was her hunger to gain answers to life's niggling questions. My mum, aunties and I all participated in this clandestine activity.

While a group of terrified yet intrigued observers huddle up in the room, three volunteers sit on the floor around the board, with their fingers placed on it gently and in the necessary manner. Soon there would be a sense of heaviness in the bodies of the three volunteers. Then, mysteriously, the board would start to vibrate. When that happened, we would attempt to ascertain the identity of the spirit by listing the names of recently deceased people or of famous individuals such as Gandhi, the world-renowned Indian activist. We would always ask the board either closed questions, to elicit a response of a number of taps for 'yes' or silence for 'no', or questions whose answer would involve a number of taps such as for a time of day or a date.

On one occasion, I asked the board if the spirit was that of my recently deceased uncle and to confirm by tapping its leg on the floor three times. That is exactly what happened. So whatever may have been the reality, our conviction at the time was that this genuinely was the departed spirit of my uncle.

I continued, asking the board, 'What time did you die?'

There followed two taps: he died at two o'clock in the night.

'How did you die? Sickness?'

Silence.

'Snake bite?'

Silence.

'Heart attack?'

Two taps. This was indeed how we believed that my uncle had died, so seemed additional confirmation that we were definitely addressing the spirit of my uncle.

'Where are you now? Are you in heaven?'

Silence.

'Are you allowed to tell us where you are?'

Silence.

'Will you be reincarnated? If yes, then tap twice.'

Two taps. My uncle would be born into a new incarnation.

The implication of this admission was crystal clear to everyone in the room that day. Even though what we believed was my uncle's spirit didn't specify where he was, all that mattered to us was that he wasn't in the place of eternal happiness. What a disappointment.

This apparent disclosure that my uncle would have to undergo another reincarnation weighed heavily on the family, but, as always, there were numerous theories to explain events. 'Well, we never really expected that he would be in heaven anyway,' was the typical, conciliatory response. But for me this revelation was yet another disaster and made me redouble my efforts to find out the answer to the pressing problem of how I could obtain a better incarnation or preferably *moksha* altogether.

Clutching at straws

Following the further disillusionment of these encounters, I increased my chanting of the name of god: 'Hari, Hari, Hari, Hari', or perhaps, 'Narayana, Narayana'. I resolved to chant them over and over again every waking moment. Of course, this meant I was absorbed in my chanting and therefore inattentive to everything else around me, something that understandably frustrated my family who could no longer easily communicate with me. It also drove them to distraction having to hear these repeated chants all day long. Only my dad wasn't too bothered, but then he was a man of very few words and was usually away at work anyway.

At times, the excessive chanting made me hallucinate. One example was during a seven-day festival of non-stop, twenty-four-hour chanting that was organised by community leaders. Anyone who wanted to could participate under the gazebo-like structure they erected. I decided to chant there for twelve hours one day, starting at 6 a.m., and then to do the same again the following day. In the middle of the second twelve-hour session, I had a hallucination. It was as if I was being transported to the heavenly abode of the god Shiva. He 'said' to me, 'I am impressed with your devotion and I want to make you a blessing for your whole family.' But he didn't ask me what I wanted. He didn't offer me anything at all.

I told my family about these experiences and they were pleased to have such a spiritual member of the family. I sensed that the gods too were pleased with me. But what really bothered and gnawed away at me was that Shiva hadn't asked me what I'd wanted – to which I would obviously have said *moksha*, or at least information about how to get there. Nor did anyone else have the decency to ask me what I wanted and why I was so dedicated to my cause.

My mum's reaction was in fact mixed. While she had a sense of happiness and pride that I was so zealous, she was frustrated that I didn't seem to be paying much attention to the normal things of the world. She was also still unhappy that I wasn't becoming a doctor, which was her utmost ambition. In fact, my mum made it abundantly clear, right up to her dying day, that she wouldn't be satisfied unless all six of her children became doctors (but not one of us did).

My second strategy to make the gods grant me assured *moksha* was prompted by the fact that I'd been told that great things can happen if somebody chanted a particular 'secret code' of verse – with sincerity and vigour, several times over – on the day of an eclipse. I was determined to do everything I could to chant this verse in the way prescribed during the next eclipse – be it solar or lunar.

During these weeks, an elderly lady came to our customary Saturday meetings. She informed me that she knew the secret herself of how to converse with the goddess Raja Rajeswari, one of the more benevolent incarnations of the wife of Shiva. I must memorise and then chant – 108 times, that special number in Hinduism – eight particular verses of the secret poetry on an eclipse day. Afterwards, the goddess herself would be ready to speak to me face to face. I asked for all the specifics of how to perform the chanting because I was determined to do it right. I wanted to master it to the extent that the idol might vibrate with life, speak with an audible voice and answer my questions. I perfected the chant, even practising it before the lady. All I had to do now was wait for the next eclipse.

Unfortunately, or so it felt at the time, I never did get the opportunity. Before the next eclipse occurred, I'd moved to Madras (now called Chennai), where the true God actually did answer my plea for information.

5

UNIVERSITY CALLS

I lived in my dad's house for nine months between spring 1965 and January 1966. During that time, I had to listen to the constant drip feed of my mum's hopeless but ever-hopeful pleading and strategising: 'Why don't you wait one more year and study harder, then maybe you can take another entrance examination to enter medical college?' Although her heart and mind were utterly set on my becoming a doctor, my mum hatched a contingency plan, unbeknown to me at the time. If – as she was beginning to realise was the case – her beloved Bhaskar was definitely never going to fulfil her Plan A, becoming a doctor, then she would have to settle for the next best course of action.

Plan B was to study engineering at the Indian Institute of Technology (or IIT), one of the most prestigious colleges in the whole of the Indian sub-continent. For this there was the option of taking a national entrance exam or a regional one. My mum had intended to apply to both, to maximise the likelihood of my being accepted. But by the time she had come up with this strategy, the application deadlines had already passed. She would have to wait another year.

With Plan B failing before it even got off the ground, my mum now deferred to Plan C. As some universities ran their academic year from January to December, rather than the usual Indian school year of May to March, she realised I could still apply to study engineering elsewhere.

The fact that my mum appeared to be not merely condoning my pursuit of engineering but actually trying to facilitate it may seem surprising. But she was influenced in no small way by a certain lady and her son. My dad had taken me to see the District Mechanical Engineer (DME) of the Indian Railways. Unexpectedly, he had assured me, 'Come back to us after your studies, Bhaskar. There will be a job ready for you in the mechanical department. You don't need to worry about your future employment. You will begin as an officer.' This unlooked-for job offer was a real encouragement to me. Later, when I told my mum about it, she informed me that the DME who made me the pledge was the son of her respected friend and fellow devotee, upon whom the spirits would often descend during religious sessions. So my mum reckoned that if this lady's son was offering me a job, then maybe that was what was meant to happen. She conceded that it was better than Plan Nothing and at least there were sufficient funds to pay for my study.

In the end, CET – the College of Engineering Technology – in Madras (some 700 miles away) accepted me as a student on its mechanical engineering programme, beginning in January 1966. My mum wasn't happy that it would be a long way from home and in a large city. She doggedly still longed for me to become a doctor. But, reluctantly, she agreed that I could go to CET on the condition that if I should somehow still manage to gain a place to study medicine, I would definitely accept it.

So, at the age of eighteen, my life was pretty much taking shape: I could finally go to university to pursue my interest in engineering, and in a respected school of study; my family were able to take care of my needs; I'd received the promise of a decent job, so my career prospects were high; there was even a young lady lined up for me to marry – my uncle's daughter. Actually, marriage was incompatible with my personal plan of eventually becoming a priest who sought *moksha*, which necessitated a celibate life. But the selection of my uncle's daughter to be my wife was my family's decision, not mine.

Except for my nagging search for *moksha*, I lacked very little. All I needed to do was to concentrate on my studies and get my degree. But that proved to be easier said than done.

To Madras and university

Going to university is often the first time a young person leaves home properly. This important rite of passage was no exception for me. Armed with a large, brass-coloured trunk, packed with all my worldly possessions, I left my sorrowful and regretful mum to her perpetual disappointment in me. I took the train to Madras and was now all alone – or, at least, that is what I thought.

Once on the train, as I was transported away from my family and my terra firma, I looked down the line to my new stage in life. Anticipation was tinged with fear. How would I ever survive without my mum's food? How would I manage in a university whose medium of teaching was a foreign tongue, English? Would the gods help me to finish my degree and enable me to be a good son to my dad? I could see how he had toiled to bring in sufficient income to support our family of eight. I genuinely wanted to graduate and then earn a good wage to support him in return. After all, that's the duty of every Indian son, especially the firstborn.

Though I was more accustomed to train travel than most Indian teenagers, those journeys had always been with my mum and my dad. Homesickness was impatiently waiting in the wings. How would I ever cope on my own?

After an emotional but otherwise uneventful seventeen-hour train journey, I arrived at Madras, in the southernmost state of India, Tamil Nadu. Madras is the sixth largest Indian city, having roughly the same population as London. It's also a whole world away from my home in its language, cuisine and culture.

Being a committed Brahmin, as soon as I arrived, I went directly to the most important temple in the city, the Parthasarathi temple, dedicated to the god Krishna. I didn't even take my belongings to my new accommodation, but first dropped them at the train's left luggage office. Once inside, I earnestly spoke to the idols there: 'I have come to this city for education, but more than that I have come seeking your help. I need to know how I can reach you when I pass from this life. Please help me.' Death is not what you'd usually expect teenagers to have at the forefront of their mind when leaving home. Having made my intentions clear to my god, I gladly retrieved my luggage and made my way to start my new life, little realising what this would actually mean.

Masala dosa but more disappointment

CET, which was affiliated to the University of Calcutta, was self-contained on its own campus. I shared a room with another student, from the state of Tamil Nadu, but I didn't see him much. There were shared toilets and showers on the corridor, but not in the same location as each other. In the orthodox Hinduism of those days, the toilet was seen as unclean and the shower as clean, so they had to be kept apart. The university hostel adhered strictly to this policy. There was also a canteen, which thankfully proved to be a source of cheer and culinary contentment, making my previous fears about Tamil food long forgotten. Madras is renowned for its exquisite cuisine. I ate three sumptuous meals a day there – all '100 per cent vegetarian'. My favourite meal was the delicious breakfast of *idli* (a steamed dumpling made of rice and lentil) and *masala dosa* (a type of pancake stuffed with spicy potato). These continued to be my favourite dishes into adulthood, as I have remained a vegetarian all my life.

Thankfully, once I arrived at university, I wasn't homesick at all. I didn't go home during the academic year because I wanted to concentrate on my studies, before returning with some laudable news of first-year success. Socialising wasn't part of my schedule – between focusing on my studying, worshiping my gods and enjoying my three tasty meals each day, I didn't have time for such superficiality, as I saw it.

The engineering degree was a four-year course. Year one was what is known as a 'studentship', which must be passed for entry to the subsequent year. My favourite aspect was calculus – I liked both the subject and the teacher. I also enjoyed trigonometry, so I must have been a closet mathematician. I was determined to do well in my degree because it was my chosen subject, rather than my mum's or anyone else's. But one's own determination doesn't necessarily ensure the successful practices of others.

There was a procedure whereby my college had to fill out a form for the registering institution (The Institute of Engineers) to record engineering students with the central organisation (Calcutta University). This was so that students could be awarded a degree from them in due course. For whatever reason, the CET office had failed to do what was necessary to list my name with the central registry in Calcutta. To my horror, I found out towards the end of my first year that I hadn't been registered and therefore the whole of my first year didn't count at all towards anything. I pleaded with the CET principal and the office administrator. Although they were apologetic, they told me I'd still have to repeat the year. Not only would this entail great disappointment for me and my family, but it would also incur enormous expenditure. I was angry and frustrated. Months of hard work and study, not to mention financial expense, had come to nothing all because of someone else's careless administration error.

Persevering, I reminded myself that having a dad who works for the Indian Railways made the whole sub-continent of India freely accessible to me. My dad sent me a rail pass for Calcutta so that I could go in person to reason with the powers that be. Maybe they would agree that I shouldn't be unfairly penalised for this arbitrary, bureaucratic mistake by a third party. But one thing that India has excessive supplies of is red tape. In spite of all my documentary evidence and pleading, and the fact I'd travelled a thousand miles to get there, they wouldn't relent. So I had to leave, battling to come to terms with the disappointment that I'd have to undertake the whole academic year all over again.

However, as I couldn't have even begun to realise then, but now emphatically understand, 'in all things God works for the good of those … who have been called according to his purpose' (Romans 8:28). These black clouds of regret actually shrouded silver linings.

Drastic measures

In those exasperated days, I was plagued by mourning for my lost year and anger about its impact on my parents. My mum was already disappointed in me for not having done medicine; I'd gone against her wishes. Now every communication from her was pestering and nagging: 'This has happened because you didn't do medicine!' (Indeed, she spent the rest of her life reminding me of this.) Even worse, my dad was now under the immense financial strain of paying for a whole wasted year of my education.

By nature, I didn't want to be an encumbrance for my parents (not that they would have necessarily seen it that way), but could do nothing to solve my dad's financial pressures. Throughout my childhood, he'd laboured single-handedly, while life had dealt bitterly with him in so many ways. In all this, I never once heard him complain, a commendable attitude I always admired in him. He took everything in his stride, even the most depressing things in life. I was devastated that now I'd be adding to his existing pressures and the enormous demands of his large family: six children plus his ageing mother. However, I could perhaps try to minimise the financial impact on my dad as much as I was able. So I moved out of the college hostel, going without those three moreish Madras meals a day, and moved into shared, self-catered lodgings.

I continued my idol worship and practices as a faithful Hindu, even though I was no longer under the auspices of my parents. My studies and a dedicated work ethic –

that had been instilled in me by parents, Akka and others – meant I had less time to give to my idols and my pursuit of answers, but my preoccupation with how to achieve *moksha* was nevertheless still present.

One Saturday, 10 September 1966, I began once again to offer earnest *puja* to the different pictures of gods and goddesses in my hostel room. I reflected that, on the one hand, I was happy that I lacked nothing tangible. On the other hand, though, I was sad about my circumstances. I was disappointed in the university administration, disappointed in myself for letting my parents down, but, in my heart of hearts, I had also to confess to being a little disappointed in my idols. The cumulative effects of all the frustrating events once again led to my pining for freedom from the labours of life, with all their relentless setbacks. I was tiring of trying my best, yet not succeeding in any of my endeavours. Not only were my efforts in this life inadequate, but all my toil ultimately was going to result in death, followed by yet another reincarnation, and so on and so on. This belief weighed my spirits down further. I must have my freedom from this endless drudgery. I craved *moksha*. Fraught, I turned again to my gods.

'I have nothing to complain about,' I said to the lifeless images on the wall of my room. 'You've given me everything. You're able to deal with this pressing problem now. But even though I'm primarily talking to you about my disappointment with the university registration, my real concern is this: please tell me what I must do to come to you after I die?'

I'd made this request countless times already up to this point. Did I really believe that the gods would ever actually answer me? Whether or not that was the case, I clearly didn't feel there was anywhere or anyone else to whom I could take my heartache.

Usually, my family and many other Hindus would worship by burning incense sticks or tablets. We would also worship gods with, among other things, flowers, milk, coconut, fruit, money and *kumkum* powder – a sacred ash made from turmeric or saffron. But that evening, perhaps driven by sheer desperation and virtual hopelessness, combined with a desire to demonstrate my wholeheartedness, I had an extraordinary compulsion to worship my gods with my own blood.

I'd never done anything like this before; in fact, I hadn't even contemplated anything similar. But driven by a lifetime of hitherto fruitless seeking, coupled with the abject regret I was experiencing, I was sure that the offering of my blood would jolt the gods into action. Where the idea sprung from, I don't know. But how could the gods remain unmoved by so great an offering as a devotee's own blood? I reasoned that this may well be for what the gods had been waiting. Clearly I hadn't done enough already to convince them of my sincerity!

So without further ado, I pricked my thumb with a safety pin. Having shed my blood, I anointed my gods sincerely with it. This was done by applying droplets of blood as marks of worship – *tikka* – on the foreheads of all the gods whose pictures hung on my wall.

With my upbringing and life's experiences, I was well accustomed to the supernatural. I'd also read many religious and mythological stories where if a devotee offered *puja* seriously and with utmost earnestness, the gods would sometimes do wonderful things in response. The Hindu scriptures supported my actions. However, I still didn't want my intense desperation and heartfelt sincerity to be lost on the gods. So anxious was I to be taken seriously and to receive a response that I was inspired to present my gods with a solemn ultimatum. Perhaps emboldened by my shedding of blood, these frank words, which I really did mean, came out of my mouth: 'If you don't tell me – tonight – how I can come to you when I die, how I can receive *moksha*, then tomorrow I will commit suicide so that I can find out for myself. I'm tired. I've kept asking and asking. I can't wait any longer. Tell me tonight how I can be released from these cycles of reincarnation – or tomorrow I will kill myself.'

Though my stipulation was genuine, I must state that I had no particular desire to die. The prospect was as horrifying as it was terrifying. But I honestly thought that the deities would be so upset that a great devotee like me would take such drastic measures, that they would spring into miraculous and spectacular action out of their sheer desperation to save me.

With heartfelt expectation, I waited for something to materialise. I was sure something appropriate would happen that evening. Surely at least one of those umpteen gods would respond to my cry?

Death is the only answer

I put my head down on my pillow on what might have been the last night of this life, but I couldn't sleep. Despite my total faith that my gods would respond accordingly by the morning, I was restless, tossing and turning in a fitful state. The hours dragged by. Proper sleep didn't come to me and neither did any of my gods. I consoled myself that I needed to be patient.

Still nothing happened. There was no supernatural event; no godly intervention; alas, no answer. All my confidence proved misplaced, and I woke up in the morning to the crushing realisation that I'd have to go through with the threat I'd made to end my own life. Or perhaps the gods needed longer to respond to me.

Sunday morning was soon long gone, then Sunday afternoon merged into Sunday evening. Now I was in a real quandary. While I didn't want to kill myself, having given my ultimatum, I didn't want to be a hypocrite or a liar either. I don't claim to have never told a lie, but I was known in my family for my trustworthiness and as one who kept his word, by and large. Moreover, I didn't want to be accused of lying over such a significant matter. Perhaps the gods were testing my sincerity. Perhaps they could argue, 'We know that you didn't actually mean what you said, therefore we won't come to your rescue.'

I couldn't retract my pledge. The gods must see me, a devotee, as a man of his word. However, perhaps there was a way to reconcile the dilemma and still give the gods a chance to act? 'Maybe I'll go one step further,' I thought. 'I'll do something that will kill me slowly so that I can see what happens before I actually die. Surely that might also give ample scope for divine intervention and my life will be spared.' As I contemplated this, I wasn't insane; I had all my wits about me. But for years, the desire for assurance and knowledge of what happens after death had been steadily building up inside me, and I was fit to burst.

So I designed my death: a slow death. I took a glass tumbler and carefully broke it. I ground it as best I could with a pestle and mortar, then mixed it into some rice I'd cooked. I reckoned that after I'd eaten the razor-sharp shards of glass, they would take their toll on my internal organs. This would allow a slow demise, thereby giving the gods time to respond to my question and save me from actually perishing.

I decisively put the lethal meal aside to be eaten that night. This would be the end of my insufferable ignorance about the afterlife. In only a matter of hours I'd discover the secret of *moksha*.

The last day of this incarnation?

Being a restless nineteen-year-old, before I ate the fatal food, I wanted to have one last walk in the city that had become my home. I always enjoyed going into the centre of Madras. So I walked absent-mindedly to the station and caught the local train into the city centre – to the unexpected encounter that would totally transform my life.

After a quarter of an hour, my train pulled in at Madras Beach station. (Despite the name, it isn't on the beach.) I wandered around aimlessly in the area known as Parry's Corner, the prominent business district renowned for its imports and exports. It was about six in the evening, so was beginning to get dark. Lights were on in shops, but workers still had two or three more hours of work to do before they could wend their way home. The humid Madras air seemed thicker and heavier than usual. Perhaps this was the last time I'd enjoy the sights and sounds of this wonderful city.

Shortly, despair began to take hold of me. My steps were heavy, but my heart was heavier. I didn't want to return to my room because I knew what I'd promised to do, or rather felt that I had to do. By now, I was hardly looking up as I walked, instead staring disconsolately at the ground. My hope that there would be some sign for me had faded with the disappearing daylight. I turned a corner to head back to Madras Beach station, only a four-minute walk away.

But while the day was getting darker, I was about to be exposed to the Light of lights. While I was preoccupied with my thoughts and with the dreadful undertaking I'd engineered for myself, I happened to pass the law courts. A man approached me and handed me something. It was a piece of paper, about the size of a postcard, printed on both sides with red ink on a white background. At the top, in English, were three words: 'Blood is needed'. I stopped in my tracks and read the first few lines written below this stark statement. It explained how a blood bank is fundamental to saving people who are dying or in desperate medical need. That title and the opening lines alone caught my attention because I'd just given my own blood to my gods at home.

In my now fluent English, I asked the man who gave me the flyer who he was. He told me his name – Jaipal Azariah – and that he was a lecturer of zoology.

I thought perhaps there must be a collection point nearby where they were in desperate need of blood donations. 'Sir, is there a blood bank here?' I asked. 'I'd like to give as much blood as you want. I don't want anything in return. I don't want to sell it. I just want to give as much as I can, for free!' I'd already heard that you could be paid about twenty rupees a bottle to give blood at that time. (I would later work for only three rupees a day, so this was no small incentive.) But I wanted to accrue as much good karma as I could, which is why I didn't want to receive any payment for my blood.

In my mind, by this I would be doing a good work, even at the point of death. I was certain the gods would be happy with my dedication to performing merit-worthy karma in my last few living minutes. Surely they would show me some consideration in my next life as a result. Good works could take anyone to heaven, I doggedly believed, and this would further bolster the plenty I already had credited to my account. Moreover, I was prepared to do the greatest good work of all, giving my own blood to save someone – and not just to a deserving or lofty person, but to a complete stranger, and for free! Surely the gods would open the door for me to heaven right there and then.

'No, it isn't a blood bank,' came the unanticipated reply. My short-lived bubble burst. 'But we are a group of teachers and students from various university colleges and we have a meeting for the public in the building here. Why don't you come in and sit down, if you have time?'

As he'd introduced himself as a university lecturer, and I'd been brought up with a great respect for teachers, I trusted him. Expecting the meeting to be either an academic one or a Hindu one, I agreed to go inside with him.

I'd never met anyone in my whole life who wasn't a Hindu or a Muslim. My mum did actually have a few close friendships with Muslims through her work as a sewing teacher. On occasion, she'd bring students home, perhaps for extra classes. They were treated like family friends. Surprising though it may sound, we welcomed the Muslim ones as much as the Hindu ones, though we'd always have to wash the cups they'd used extra well afterwards. Nor were we allowed to eat the food they so generously brought to share with us.

Even then, relationships between Hindus and Muslims could be tense. I vividly remember the horrific scenes of dead bodies in the street during the Pakistan–India war of 1965. Such was the distrust between the groups around that time that if any Muslim was seen in a predominantly Hindu locality, he or she was as risk of being murdered by Hindu mobs. One night during this period, two of my mum's Muslim students were at our house when she forbade them to leave, saying their lives would be threatened by Hindus outside if they did so. They accepted sanctuary with us. The next day, we escorted them to the railway station, but only after we had put the *bindi* (a coloured dot or mark) on their forehead to make them look like Hindus. Muslim men at that time even had to resort to shaving their beards just so they could pass as Hindus and thereby save their lives. It was a terrible and shameful time in my country's history, but I am thankful that my parents nevertheless taught me respect for our Muslim friends.

However, I'd never met a Christian. I certainly hadn't even heard the name of Jesus Christ until then. In my family and community, as was the predominant attitude in India, the label 'Christian' was equated with a particular ethnic group: 'Anglo-Indians'. These were the offspring of white British invaders and their indigenous Indian partners, producing children of dual heritage. That generation's behaviour was perceived, stereotypically, as immoral and counter-cultural for marriage-centred societies such as ours. So, unfortunately, not only did 'Anglo-Indian' become synonymous with 'Christian', but both became synonymous with immoral lifestyles. It pains me now that this is still an issue in India today, further exacerbated by the predominance of Western media that shows the unbiblical practices and attitudes of westerners from so-called Christian countries. All this gives Jesus Christ and His followers a wicked and unjustified reputation.

Up to that evening, I had no notion whatsoever about the nature of true Christianity. When Mr Azariah cheerfully escorted me into the building, I unwittingly sat down in a Christian meeting, little realising what I was about to encounter.

THE MOST SIGNIFICANT REVELATION OF MY LIFE

I was intrigued to know what kind of meeting a university professor would invite me to where blood was required but not for a blood bank. Thoughts of the horrific meal awaiting my return home were temporarily replaced by curiosity at my new surroundings. These were my first steps into a Christian building, a church. I remember entering an unassuming hall, with a table on either side of the doorway on which were various pieces of literature. A few benches were facing the front of the room. There were probably only a handful of other people dotted around the room – all men, as it happened.

There were a few songs led by a man at the front, and some other people joined in with singing. I didn't pay attention to the words, though it was probably the first time I'd heard English being sung. After the music, another teacher stood up at the front to speak. I don't remember most of what he said, except that every so often he repeated the same sentence: 'Believe in the Lord Jesus Christ and you will have eternal life.' That got my attention – specifically, the little word 'will'. The man wasn't saying, 'might', or 'perhaps', or 'maybe', or 'possibly – as long as you do enough good works'. Neither was he saying, 'hopefully', or, 'This is one of the many ways available.' He was unapologetically and dogmatically stating, 'You *will* have eternal life.'

I didn't know who Jesus Christ was. Curious to rectify my ignorance, at the end of the meeting I asked Mr Azariah, 'Who is this Jesus Christ that man was talking about?'

'What is your name?'

'My name is Bhaskar. I am an engineering student and I come from a priestly family,' I respectfully replied, before asking, 'Which incarnation is this Jesus Christ?'

'What do you mean?' Mr Azariah responded, looking puzzled.

'Sir,' I said, 'I know all the stories about the ten incarnations of the Hindu god Vishnu like the back of my hand, but I have never heard this name before.' (According to the Hindu scriptures, nine incarnations have already taken place, with the tenth one due when the world comes to an end.)

By way of answer, Mr Azariah showed me Christ directly: 'Well, I may not be able to explain in detail now, but I can do something for you. I can show you my religious book. Something here might be of interest.' So he opened his religious book – which, of course, I now know to be the Bible – and read the world's most famous Bible verse: 'For God so loved the world that he gave his one and only Son, that whoever believes in him shall not perish but have eternal life' (John 3:16). Mr Azariah then suggested to me that the verse could be read slightly differently: 'For God so loved *Bhaskar*, that he gave his only Son for *Bhaskar*, that if *Bhaskar* believes in him, *Bhaskar* shall not perish but *Bhaskar* will have eternal life.'

When I heard the verse read this way, it had an electrifying effect on me. I was flabbergasted because the whole emphasis was shifted: my future was not determined by *my* endeavours, or *my* devotion, or *my* religion, or *my* observance, or *my* labour, or *my* chanting, or *my* karma, or *my* pilgrimages, or *my* fasting. Someone else was in the driving seat; someone else could give eternal life. Not only did I want to be saved, but here I was being told in plain language that God wanted to save me! God had even gone so far as to execute a plan to that end. The initiative and the effort were shifted from me to God. It was God who loved, God who gave, God who wanted me not to perish.

This is the gloriously liberating truth of the gospel of grace, which is the core message of Christianity. It's also the polar opposite of what I'd been taught until then. It moved the whole emphasis of my mindset and gave me a sense of excited relief to know that my efforts (and presumably my blood) weren't necessary after all. No wonder all my religious practices hadn't yielded the answers for which I'd longed.

'Let me pray for you,' Mr Azariah continued. I thought that 'pray' might be the English word for some kind of religious ceremony, so when he bowed his head, I followed him. When he prayed, he spoke out to Someone I couldn't see. I wondered where his God was. Surely there should be some kind of physical icon – an idol or picture – to focus upon? I was curious to see whether Mr Azariah could actually reach his God in this manner that was totally alien to me.

But when Mr Azariah prayed, something remarkable happened. I had an undeniable feeling that Someone was standing next to me, removing a heavy, intolerable burden from my back and throwing it away. It wasn't a vision or suchlike, but an immense, real feeling. I felt incredibly light and free. I felt overjoyed that this transformation was all God's work, not mine. What's more, this revelation was prompted by God's love for me, not by my devotion, or religion, or good works. And it was given positively and definitively: I, Bhaskar, *will* have eternal life. As I noted on my watch, this took place at exactly 7.50 in the evening on Sunday 11 September 1966 – at St Andrew's Church on Parry's Corner.

While nothing happened to me physically – and I still had problems to deal with – something tangible and life-changing had happened within me. This revelation that I couldn't be saved by my own efforts must have been why, despite years of heartfelt effort and religious toil, I still hadn't received any reassurance of *moksha*.

Beginning with the Bible

I returned home jubilantly that night, clutching a Gideon's New Testament (the second part of the Bible) that I'd been given as I left the meeting. With extreme relief, I threw away the deadly meal I'd prepared. I'd been given the answer I so desperately wanted. 'The gods' had spoken, finally. I was yet to grasp the uniqueness of Jesus Christ, though, and was still trying to fit Him into my Hindu mindset. So I declared gratefully to the photographs of the gods in front of me, 'I don't know who You are, but I heard about You today. You have a strange name that I have never heard before, but the man who spoke to me says if I believe in You, You will give me the assurance of eternal life. Seeing as I've tried so many other things, I don't mind trying You as well.'

That week, I went to my scheduled college lectures and study, but, for the first time in my life, I did *not* worship my idols, as had been my daily practice. Feeling that I was now on a more fruitful path, instead I spent the intervening days trying to read my English New Testament. Not surprisingly, I started right at the beginning with the Gospel of Matthew. The version that I read at the time begun like this,

The book of the generation of Jesus Christ, the son of David, the son of Abraham. Abraham begat Isaac; and Isaac begat Jacob; and Jacob begat Judas and his brethren; and Judas begat Phares and Zara of Thamar; and Phares begat Esrom; and Esrom begat Aram; and Aram begat Aminadab; and Aminadab begat Naasson; and Naasson begat Salmon ...

Well, not only were these foreign-sounding names a little tricky, but I had no idea whatsoever what 'begat' meant – after all, I'd been given the Authorised King James translation, dating from 1611. I almost gave up, due to the confusing language and foreign concepts. But my difficulties and frustrations in trying to read it were somehow surpassed by the weight of my desire for answers and insight.

The following Sunday evening couldn't arrive quickly enough and I eagerly returned to St Andrew's Church. Mr Azariah was thrilled to see that I'd returned, and I was warmly welcomed. I was more relaxed than I'd been the previous week. The meeting had a similar format to the week before. Afterwards, I was told that in a month's time some of the students would be going for a weekend camp in Tinnanur, twenty miles outside of Madras. I was invited to join them and assured that I'd be taken care of, so agreed to go. (Later, I learnt that these were college students and teachers belonging to a Christian group called the Union of Evangelical Students of India (UESI), which was itself part of the International

Fellowship of Evangelical Students (IFES), a worldwide Christian organisation.)

In the meantime, on hearing about the trouble I was having with reading the Gospel of Matthew, someone at the church suggested that I start instead with the fourth book of the New Testament: the Gospel of John. That was more accessible, even in the Authorised King James Version:

In the beginning was the Word, and the Word was with God, and the Word was God. The same was in the beginning with God. All things were made by Him; and without Him was not anything made that was made. In Him was life; and the life was the light of men. And the light shineth in darkness; and the darkness comprehended it not.

I was also given a book about someone called George Müller.

Over the four weeks until the camp, I read both the Gospel of John and the Müller book, and was fascinated by both. It didn't take me long to reach John 3:16: 'For God so loved the world, that he gave his only begotten Son, that whosoever believeth in him should not perish, but have everlasting life' (KJV). That was a real highlight for me in those early days of reading the Bible. Though I still didn't fully understand its significance, I was beginning to see that this teaching was radically different from that of Hinduism. I was also impressed by the story of George

Müller's life. His trust and faith in God enabled him to provide for over 2000 orphans who were in his care. Müller's policy was to never ask another human being for help: he would only ever share his needs with God through prayer. This was a practice that so struck me that it set a pattern for my life. I wanted to follow Müller's example.

A dramatic and definitive answer

On Friday 21 October 1966, five weeks after my first meeting with genuine Christians, I travelled with my new-found companions by train to the camp. It was held in St Bain's School. There were fourteen students (girls and boys), three teachers and three speakers in attendance. What was lovely was how they accepted me just as I was into their number. They didn't refer to my Hinduism. Neither did they suggest that I had to become a Christian. They even paid for all my camp expenses so that I wasn't in any way disadvantaged.

On Saturday, we had meetings all day, which the three speakers took turns to lead. The talks were engaging and accessible. The students were considerate, helping me to find my way around the Christian Scriptures. We also sang songs, two of which stuck in my mind. The first went, 'Rolled away, rolled away, now the burden of my sin has rolled away.'[5] The second, which has since become like an anthem to me, declared, 'I have decided to follow Jesus … no turning back, no turning back'.[6]

Towards the end of the camp, on Sunday afternoon, the students, teachers and speakers sat on chairs in a circle and held what they called 'a time of testimony', where each person shared an account of something God had done for them. I was surprised to hear each of them bear testimony to a personal encounter with Him. This was a completely foreign concept for me. Some said that God had spoken to them, some that God had blessed them, others that God had shown them something. They were using the name of God as if they actually knew Him personally, closely, intimately.

I viewed all of this with a sense of perplexed curiosity mixed with indignation. I'd come from a conservative and orthodox Hindu family. We didn't utter the name of a god if we were wearing shoes. We didn't speak the name of a god if we were wearing the clothes in which we'd been to the toilet. We didn't sit on chairs when worshipping god, but on the floor or preferably prostrating ourselves before him. In fact, I always used to get into trouble because I tended to chant the name of a god at any time, in any place, in any situation, whatever my outward condition and circumstances. There were times when my mum would even throw things at me while I was dishonouring the traditional method of being holy and consecrated before uttering the name of a Hindu god.

But I saw these people were wearing shoes and sitting on chairs. I knew some of them weren't ritually clean. Yet, they were speaking of God as if He belonged to them and was somehow close to them. I had no choice but to conclude that they were lying: there was no way that God would have had any personal dealings with unclean people like that.

The campers continued to speak of the work of God in their lives. One of the speakers was no less than an Indian army official, Captain Raja Ratnam. I reasoned silently and resignedly to myself that if someone as distinguished as him were to present one of these things called a testimony, I might believe what they were saying. Just as I was harbouring these thoughts, Captain Ratnam stood up and shared things that God had done in his life. He was followed by the other two main speakers. That really unsettled me. Even the teachers – who in my mind were equal to priests – claimed such intimacy and nearness to God that they could hear His very voice personally. Compared to my superbly devout Bojja Tata, who was obsessed with his ritual cleanliness, these men were utterly filthy. Nevertheless, they seemed to have a level of relationship with God that was mystifying yet compelling, to say the least. This presented a great conflict in my mind, and gave birth to a new question: what do these men have that I seem to lack?

I didn't have to contemplate this for too long. Without warning, while I was pondering these matters deeply, I distinctly heard these words: 'Stand up and speak.' They were loud and clear, and spoken directly to me, yet I couldn't identify the source. I asked the people sitting next to me whether they had said anything, but they hadn't. Bewildered, I tried to ignore what I was sure I had heard. I attempted to gather my thoughts, but to no avail. They came a second time: 'Stand up and speak.' Shaken, again I asked those around me whether they had addressed me, but they adamantly denied having said anything. I was troubled and restless. I wasn't imagining things; I had definitely heard something. But who was it? Was it a practical joke? I wasn't going to stand up and I certainly wasn't going to speak! Again, I didn't have to wait long. After a moment, the voice once more commanded me, 'Stand up and speak!' It was more insistent and unambiguous. I was so scared that, with some sort of mumbled excuse, I left the group. I figured that the only place I could go where I wouldn't be followed was, oddly enough, the toilet – a most unclean place for a Brahmin like me. So I escaped there and locked the door.

Rattled, I tried to compose myself and to rationalise what I'd experienced. It didn't make sense. Who was speaking to me in this clear and audible voice that I couldn't identify? Why were these Christians so different from me? Why couldn't I justify or emulate the claims I'd heard them make? What did these Christians have that I didn't have? I was confounded by these mysteries; I was completely out of my depth. I didn't know what was happening to me; it was all so overwhelming. My legs weakened as any strength seemed to drain out of me. I had to sit down – on the toilet floor!

Suddenly and strangely, everything around me seemed to change. I was neither asleep nor daydreaming, but had the feeling of being engulfed by a red liquid. It was crimson coloured. In fact, it looked like blood, and I felt like I was being completely immersed in it. I didn't know where the liquid was coming from, but I felt the urge to look above. Peering upwards, I saw a wooden beam in a cross-like structure. From it I saw drops of blood pouring into the flow in which I was immersed. I was terrified and needed an explanation.

As if by way of response, and as suddenly as it had begun, I received a crystal-clear feeling. I can't identify the exact nature of the revelation – it may have been an audible voice. But it was concrete: definite, distinct and personal. The voice said to me, 'You need *My* blood; I don't need yours. It is *My* blood that will make you like the people out there who are testifying.'

I perceived this statement as clearly as if someone had physically and discernibly explained it to me. This was so much so that I even responded in return, 'What is it that these people have that I don't have, that I can't speak about God like they do, as if they know Him personally, even though they are ritually unclean?'

The explanation was immediately provided: 'You need Me and My blood.'

In all my years of asking countless unanswered questions, here I'd asked a single question and had received the answer without hesitation.

'Lord, I accept,' I replied. At that moment, everything became normal again. I was still in the toilet. It was broad daylight. I looked down at my clothes. I wasn't covered in blood. It was 3.45 p.m. on Sunday 23 October 1966.

Baffled, I emerged from the cubicle. At first, I wondered whether the students had mixed something intoxicating into my food, as this whole experience had come out of the blue. It was strange but nevertheless real. I didn't tell anyone what had happened, but kept it to myself – after all, who would I tell and who would believe me? I knew sooner or later I'd have to tell my parents something, but definitely not yet. Even I didn't understand, so what could I have said to them?

A new direction

I'd now attended church for six Sunday evenings, been reading a Gideon's New Testament and had even gone to a Christian camp. There was still much I needed to learn about this newfound faith, but I did know from day one that the Christian message was diametrically different from Hinduism. I was so used to superstition, magic, astrology and other (I now realise) occult practices. The Christian faith is built on truth, peace, mercy and openness. The God of the Bible is the One who made the universe and sustains it. He has set the example of how we should live, through his Son, Jesus Christ. He took the initiative to send Jesus into the world to save people from their sins, once and for all. The Christian life is not based on rules and rituals, but on a personal relationship with the living God. Yes, it should involve the discipline of daily Bible reading and prayer, but that is borne out of gratitude for God's grace and the desire to be more like Him each day. The Christian's desire to be holy and upright isn't because their salvation from hell depends on it; it's because they know they're guaranteed a place in heaven through the sacrifice of Jesus on the cross, and thus are free from fear to live a life that honours God and demonstrates His goodness to others. It is Jesus' blood that made all this possible.

The Christians I knew were distinct in the content of their teaching and in the character of their behaviour. They had no idols at all. They were attached to only one book of Scripture: the Bible. They had no ritualistic regulations. During the time I'd spent with them, they hadn't revealed any bad habits and their language was clean. Above all, as I've mentioned before, what struck me most was that they seemed to know their God personally.

Thanks to my compelling experience at camp, I did now begin to appreciate something of the uniqueness of this God. When I returned from Tinnanur to my student hostel, I made, by God's grace, a definite break away from my Hindu gods. I knew enough to understand that the God of the Bible was a different God altogether. Although I hadn't exactly worshipped my idols since 11 September, they'd still been there on the wall of my room and in the back of my mind. But after that experience in the toilet at camp, the idols lost their hold on me. I felt a wonderful sense of freedom. It was as if I was able to shake off the fetters that had bound me to my idols. I didn't even bring to mind the threats I'd heard all my life about the revenge the gods would wreak on any so-called follower who failed to worship them religiously. Thankfully, my struggle was no longer with my deities, although I would continue fighting against the superstitions that were so deeply engrained into my psyche and practice, and which pervade every level of Indian society.

This ongoing battle against superstitions was exemplified within three days of returning from camp. I'd just left my accommodation to attend the day's lectures when – most inconveniently – I heard a loud sneeze from somewhere. This stopped me dead in my tracks. Hearing or having a sneeze when leaving your house is a bad omen. Previously, I would have gone back inside immediately, had some water and sat down, waiting for the omen to pass before attempting to leave the house again. I stood frozen, caught between my old life and my new one. How could I go forward without some calamity befalling me? Just as this horrifying dilemma was going through my mind, the chorus that I'd learnt at camp came to me: 'I have decided to follow Jesus … no turning back, no turning back.' That was the answer. 'Thank you, Jesus,' I said in my heart. 'I will go forward and not turn back.' And so I stepped out in faith and confidence, knowing that I was now a follower of Christ.

NEW LIFE IN CHRIST; NO TURNING BACK

For the next two weeks, as I attended college and read the New Testament, the implications of this radical change in my life reverberated in my head. I couldn't escape the remarkable fact that on the very same weekend that I'd shed my own blood to anoint the pictures of my Hindu idols, a complete stranger had handed me a flyer with 'blood' printed on it. A few weeks later, I'd had the striking sensation of blood flowing from a crossbeam above and immersing me – so unlike any other spiritual experience I'd had before. When I'd thought that my blood needed to be shed, my heavenly Father had intervened – before I did myself any permanent damage – to tell me that Jesus' blood had already been shed to save sinners like me. Since then, I have often marvelled at how personalised God's outreach to me was – His was a custom-made intervention in my life, unique and individualised. The God of the Bible knows us intimately and in love. 'God moves in a mysterious way, His wonders to perform', as William Cowper aptly worded it in his hymn.

A fortnight after camp, and therefore two weeks into my new Christian life, the speaker at church on Sunday evening was called Mr Mohan. Afterwards, I was introduced to him as someone who was 'interested in the gospel'. He asked me, 'Where do you go for worship?' I didn't know – I'd never heard the word 'worship' used like this before and didn't go anywhere to do it as far as I knew.

'Those of us who believe in Jesus Christ usually meet together on Sunday mornings as well as Sunday evenings,' he explained. 'We have a time of thinking about God and listening to what the Bible says.' I hadn't developed the habit of going anywhere on a Sunday morning.

'Why don't you come to my church, next Sunday morning?' he asked, giving me the details. He wasn't pushy, but was hopeful that I'd accept his invitation. This would prove to become a strong and enduring friendship. The funny thing is that at this point he was encouraging me in my faith, but in later years it would be the other way round.

The following week, I duly made my way to Emmanuel Methodist Church, Vepery. Compared to my experience at St Andrew's, this was a big church – there were perhaps 300 people there, in a long, thin hall. Compared to the students who had been at St Andrew's, this congregation also seemed to be wealthy. I considered how I must have looked to them: a lean student who didn't even have shoes to wear, only rubber *chappals* (flip-flops). But I swallowed my pride and, in fear and trembling, went into the room.

In its format, the service at Emmanuel was similar to ones at St Andrew's, but slightly more formal. After the service had finished, Mr Mohan came over to welcome me. Then he took me to meet someone who they called 'Pastor' – the leader of the church, Pastor Kamaleson. I was amazed that someone so important had the time to speak to me and this made an instant, positive impression on me. He seemed so welcoming and was so confident, natural and concerned that any apprehensions I'd had that morning soon dissipated. Next, Mr Mohan presented me to an elderly gentleman who spoke my Telugu language; his name was Mr Giri.

I remember to this day that when I was introduced to Mr Giri, he shook me by both my hands and, looking straight into my eyes, demanded to know, 'Have you been baptised?' I was taken aback, not least because I had no idea what he was talking about. 'You must be baptised', he persisted, 'because I delayed baptism for several years and regret that I didn't do so earlier. You should be baptised as soon as you can.'

That same day, Mr Giri virtually dragged me to the pastor (again!), saying, 'Arrange a baptismal service for this young man.' While I had no understanding what baptism was or what its significance was, in my naïve sincerity I wanted to do it. It must be important, judging by the response of the well-meaning people around me.

The pastor listened with concern, then respectfully replied, 'Mr Giri, if you say so, I'll do it.' I think the pastor must have known Mr Giri's regret about having put off his own baptism for many years. As it turned out, my baptism was not quite that straightforward.

Mr Giri

Mr Giri's full name was Sattiraju Sesha Giri, but, as is common in south India where most people have long, polysyllabic names and surnames, he shortened it to SS Giri. As his name suggested, he'd been born not only into a Hindu family but into the priestly Brahmin caste, like me. He'd married while still a Hindu, but his wife had become paralysed following a stroke. When some Christians had prayed for her, God had wonderfully healed her. Being a doctor, Mrs Giri struggled to accept that this healing hadn't been wrought by human intervention. However, through the catalyst of this gracious physical healing, eventually she became a Christian, followed by her daughter, Ratna. In time, Mr Giri and his two sons also became followers of Christ.

Mr Giri was a prestigious man. He had worked all his life at the Life Insurance Corporation (LIC) and had retired as principal of the LIC training college for development officers. He was also the son-in-law to the vice-chancellor of Madras University. His daughter, Ratna, was married to Madhav Rao, who also worked at LIC. They both lived in the Giri household. As I came to know Madhav better over the years, I found him to be upright and godly.

The warm welcome I received from this family, who took me under their wings, was a significantly important aspect of my early days of being a Christian. God had provided a safe haven for me without me even asking for it or recognising how important it would be for me. Though I was in Madras, a different state from my own with its distinct language and culture, God had provided a family of Hindu-Brahmin background who spoke my language, who had become Christians and who would have implicit understanding to empathise with my situation.

Once again, God had a custom-built plan for my individual situation. The family's genuine welcome and unconditional acceptance of me are things for which I am eternally grateful. As I look back now, I realise that this constituted my early training in Christian discipleship. Warm, persevering and loving hospitality speaks volumes.

My new Sunday routine

I began to go to Emmanuel Methodist Church regularly. I attended both the young people's Bible group on Fridays and the young people's Sunday school which took place after the service on Sunday mornings. Following this, I went with most of my fellow students from the UESI to Jehovah Shammah (meaning 'God is there' in Hebrew), a short walk just down the road. This was one of many church assemblies started all over India by Bhakht Singh, a Punjabi convert from Sikhism. As Emmanuel met early in the morning, even the young people's meeting would finish by 10.30 or 11, around when the Jehovah Shammah assembly would begin. That meant I could attend two churches on a Sunday morning. I was hungry to devour as much of the Bible being taught as I possibly could.

Attendance at church is nothing like attendance at a Hindu temple. A Hindu, when entering the temple, needs to announce to the god that he is coming by ringing the bell that is outside the door. He needs to impress upon the god that he is entering with humility by touching the steps with his hand. He can't enter the temple with his shoes on. He must never enter the temple without external offerings, such as banana and coconut. The Hindu can only worship in front of a physical idol, and is not allowed to show his back or feet to the idol. He must communicate his farewell to the gods by ringing the bell on his way out.

There is very little communal element to Hindu worship. Instead, it is predominately individual, with the devotee coming and going as he or she pleases during any of the temple's opening hours. Sometimes a priest will engage with an individual worshipper, perhaps by passing on a physical blessing such as a *prasad* sweet that has been offered to the god. But the Hindu priest will rarely address a congregation or collection of worshippers. Even at weddings, the priest only addresses the immediate participants in the marriage ceremony.

Christian churches, on the other hand, are fundamentally different. Attendance at church is at a set time on a set day because it's communal. Christians understand that they are the body of Christ, not just isolated individuals. They can come just as they are regardless of what they are wearing or how they stand. They don't need to announce to God that they are coming into church because He already knows:

You know when I sit and when I rise;
you perceive my thoughts from afar.
You discern my going out and my lying down;
you are familiar with all my ways.

(Psalm 139:2–3)

Not only do they not need a physical object to worship, but any kind of idol would be insulting to the God who created heaven and earth. The pastor helps everyone to have a focused, unified time of worship together and a mutual period of learning about God as He is revealed in the Bible.

Jehovah Shammah had two or three speakers, invariably followed by something called Holy Communion. Jesus taught His followers this simple ceremony of remembrance just before He died on the cross. It recalls the key truths of the Christian gospel: that Jesus died as a substitutionary sacrifice to pay the punishment our sins deserve, before rising again three days later to show that His sacrifice had been sufficient.

Christians participate in Communion by eating a small piece of bread and by drinking a sip of grape juice or wine (usually a non-alcoholic type in India and many other places). Initially, I was horrified that everyone in the meeting would take a sip from the same cup. This went against my upbringing, not least because all these people were non-Brahmins from different backgrounds and classes. But I came to understand that, according to the Bible, there are only two categories of people in God's eyes. The first are those who are sinners who have *not* accepted the gift of forgiveness for their sins that is freely, graciously and mercifully offered by Jesus' death. They therefore continue to be unholy and impure in God's eyes. The second are those who were sinners – as they will continue to be until God perfects them in heaven – but *have* accepted God's free gift of forgiveness through Jesus' substitutionary death on the cross. If God saw people from different classes and backgrounds as equal, then I must do the same.

It did cross my mind that had any of my own family witnessed this 'equality', they would have been rather disconcerted. But I hadn't yet told them anything of my new faith, and without social media in those days, they would remain ignorant for now. I continued to put any thought of informing my family to the back of my mind, not wanting to consider the perturbing ramifications for my family or me.

On Sunday afternoons, the Jehovah Shammah church provided a free meal for everyone, which I'd eat gratefully – it was a real incentive to attend. I was then often invited back to people's homes for the afternoon, before returning to Jehovah Shammah for the evening service. This full Sunday spent with other Christians helped me in the steep learning curve of my new faith. It was also an oasis in the spiritual desert of the rest of my week, something with which many Christians around the world will be able to identify.

Considering the inevitable

I'd become increasingly aware that Christianity, a totally different faith from Hinduism, would have serious implications for my life. I was beginning to understand – though vaguely – that my parents would be angry and upset, to say the least, when they eventually heard about my new faith. But I'd need to tell them sooner or later, and preferably sooner rather than later. I'd now been a Christian for about two months. The question was when and how to tell my parents this life-changing news. Furthermore, what would happen to me when I told them? What would happen to my relationship with them? Would I even still have a family afterwards? These were disturbing questions, as any convert to Christianity will know.

I considered my situation. What would happen to me was of primary importance because I was completely financially dependent on my parents at that time. I knew that Madras wouldn't be my home forever; a job and a bride were still waiting for me at Bondamunda, though my Christian faith suggested that neither of these would be realistic options any more. Another consideration that weighed heavily on me was what would happen to my dad when he heard the news. I would certainly be rejected by my family for becoming a Christian, even being treated as if I were dead to them. As such, I would not be able to contribute to the family pot in the future to support them.

I was the eldest son – how would they manage without my income? My dad would have to work even harder for the next decade or so. A nauseating feeling arose within me. This was going to be too painful for all of us.

I would only be able to tell them with God's help. I sank to my knees in prayer, asking for two things. Firstly, no matter what the outcome, I prayed that God would help me not to ask anyone for financial support. Influenced by the George Müller book I had read, I understood that the God I worshipped was the same God who provided for all 2000 orphans under Müller's care. I wanted to put this faith and trust into action. Secondly, I prayed for help for my dad that he wouldn't suffer more due to my decision to follow Christ.

At one time, I thought that I'd simply go home, inform them of my new way of life, receive their reluctant blessing, say farewell to my parents and then go onward in my Christian walk. But while I pondered these things, I read this in Luke's Gospel: 'No one who puts a hand to the plough and looks back is fit for service in the kingdom of God' (Luke 9:62). They were the words of Jesus Himself to a would-be follower. For the second time, the song lyrics 'no turning back' struck me. I would have to take the full consequences of this new life, regardless of what my family may think of or do to me.

An outward sign of an inward change

Not surprisingly, I had received various well-meaning advice and counsel from my Christian friends. The common recommendation was that I should wait until I was baptised before telling my family. Most of them suggested avoiding my family as much as possible until then because they were concerned that my family might threaten me, shaking my new faith. Despite my initial dilemma – wanting to be with my family, but afraid to do so – I accepted the advice to first wait until I was baptised. That would mean another six months of my parents being unaware of my dramatic change, as I will explain.

One thing that has struck me about the early days of my newfound faith is that Christianity has a jargon all of its own. The vocabulary is like a whole new language to anyone exposed to it for the first time. There are long, technical words such as 'sanctification', 'justification' and 'substitutionary atonement'. Other terms – like 'God', 'prayer' and 'worship' – are used by religions the world over, but have a unique meaning in Christianity. I felt as if I was scrambling around in the dark, trying to work out whether prayer and worship were practised in the same manner as in Hinduism – which, of course, they are not. 'Baptism' was another puzzling concept, ever since Mr Giri first mentioned it to me.

Baptism, according to the New Testament, is the immersion of a Christian believer into water. It comes from the Greek word *baptizo* meaning 'immersion'. (Greek is the language in which the New Testament was originally written.) The Bible makes it clear that baptism doesn't clean you whatsoever to make you acceptable by God. It also makes it unmistakably plain that human beings can do nothing whatsoever to contribute to their own salvation – that is, people cannot save themselves from God's right, just anger at their sin. Salvation is all the work of God's grace. Salvation comes only by an individual accepting that Jesus Christ paid for their sins through His death on the cross. Baptism is therefore an outward sign subsequent to an inward change. It's a public declaration or visual aid to demonstrate that the person has become a Christian and wishes to be publicly identified with Christ. Jesus Christ Himself was baptised as an example to us.

In places such as India, baptism is viewed as part and parcel of your actual conversion, similar to the practices of New Testament times. Hindu, Sikh or Muslim parents whose child has become a Christian generally don't become too concerned with a merely verbal testimony. It's the physical act of baptism that seals the new faith in their thinking. This is so much the case that families will think that if they can prevent their son's or daughter's baptism, then they won't have left the family's faith after all. Thus baptism holds a strong and convincing message in these environments.

As I mentioned earlier, Mr Giri took me to Pastor Kamaleson about being baptised my first Sunday at Emmanuel Methodist Church. It was arranged that I would be baptised the following Sunday – 18 December 1966. I was keen to undertake this sign of commitment to my new faith as soon as possible. I especially looked forward to that Sunday all week, and could hardly wait to go through the waters of baptism just as my Saviour Himself had done two thousand years previously.[7]

But two days before the scheduled date for the baptism, the pastor phoned me to ask how old I was. With disappointment building as I already anticipated his response, I replied that I was in my twentieth year. He then explained that, having contacted some legal experts, he was reluctant to baptise me because I was under twenty-one. Though legally I might have been classed as an adult, culturally I was still a child. The pastor, fearing possible reprisals from my dad, said that I would have to wait until my twenty-first year. I was distraught, but there was nothing I could do about it.

Two days later, I witnessed someone else being baptised, while I'd been denied that opportunity. Next to the water tank I wept bitterly. Why couldn't I do the same? I was overwhelmed. Nor was I embarrassed to show my emotion in front of the whole church. The pastor climbed out of the baptistery – the special outdoor bath used for full immersion – and, still wearing his wet clothes, lovingly hugged me in front of the whole congregation. 'I tell you here and now, Bhaskar, that the Sunday after your birthday, I will baptise you. Please forgive me for not being able to do it today.' I was somewhat consoled by this and longed for the time, six months later, when I could hopefully look forward to more than just my birthday.

God's provision in practice

In many countries, Christmas – the celebration of Jesus'

physical birth as a baby in Bethlehem, Israel – is the biggest festival in the calendar. Nevertheless, I'd had no concept of it until December 1966, when the other young people at Emmanuel discussed their Christmas plans: 'I'll be getting clothes.' 'I'm going to be given a new suit.' 'We're going to Darjeeling to visit my aunty.' Being an affluent church, they celebrated Christmas by giving and receiving gifts, and by visiting friends and family. But I had no one in that city to share gifts with or to visit as such. While I didn't suffer financially, I didn't have excess money to spend on non-essentials.

However, one of the members of the church, a middle-aged man I barely knew who was a doctor by profession, asked me to accompany him to a shop. He said he was looking at fabrics to order some trousers and a shirt for himself. 'How do you like these?' he asked.

'They will suit you well – they are nice,' I politely replied.

'No, they're not for me, they're for you! I want to give you a Christmas present,' he explained. I was taken aback. Then he continued, 'Would you like to come to our house on Saturday, Christmas Eve? You're on your own; why not come and spend time with us?' I gratefully accepted this generous invitation as I was still living in my student accommodation and would otherwise have been on my own.

By now I was accustomed to the kindness and hospitality of Christians. Many of them were adept at making me feel like part of their family. Some of them even said that I was free to come to their house at any time I liked, which seemed amazing to me. At home, we weren't habitually hospitable to anyone who wasn't part of the family, although – as I mentioned earlier – we did on occasions receive Muslim visitors. But my Christian friends treated me as if I were family and afforded me the liberties that this implied. Again, Christian hospitality speaks volumes.

During the week running up to Christmas, it so happened that my only belt broke. I had just enough money to buy a replacement, so went to a shop and bought a new one. But, annoyingly, the next morning as I was trying to put it on, the new belt broke as well. I didn't have any more money and felt sorry that I'd broken two belts in as many days. I'd just have to make do without one for now.

On Christmas Eve, I went to this welcoming doctor's house. They had an artificial tree in their room, bedecked with bright and shiny decorations, and surrounded by gifts. The children received toys, the doctor was given some stationery and his wife was given a fancy hair accessory. Then they called my name to present me with a gift. I was surprised because they'd already given me material for trousers and a shirt, as well as inviting me that day for a meal and warmly welcoming me. But, intrigued, I took the package and opened it expectantly. I had a real shock (in the good sense of the word): it contained a beautiful, good-quality belt, which was exactly what I needed.

That impressed upon me that God is aware of my specific needs and He can take better care of me than I can.

What wonderful care the Lord takes of His people, even in the small, mundane things of life. Indeed, Luke 12:6 states, 'Are not five sparrows sold for two pennies? Yet not one of them is forgotten by God.' Already, I was finding this to be true in my life.

Sustained in struggle

As I grew in my Christian faith and as I considered the consequences of my decision to follow the Lord Jesus Christ, I continued to be aware that the day my dad and mum came to know of this would put me in a difficult situation spiritually, emotionally and financially. I presumed they would refuse to give me financial support unless I came back home and renounced my newfound faith. So I resolved to find myself a job.

One day, I was cycling home from college along Mount Road, an area with many offices. Out of nowhere, but very distinctly, a voice said to me, 'Go and meet the brother who works in the Fisheries Department: Mr Abraham.' There was no other person around me who could have uttered these words. But the instruction was clear: meet the Assistant Director of Fisheries for the Madras government, who was also from Jehovah Shammah and a Christian 'brother'.

I turned off the road, arrived at the correct building and parked my bike. I wasn't entirely sure what would happen or how I'd be received when I entered the office. I simply asked the secretary to tell Mr Abraham that Bhaskar Rao was here to see him. (Bhaskar Rao is how most people knew me, given that Bhaskararao Sreerangam is quite a mouthful.)

'I can't believe this,' announced Mr Abraham, clasping my hands in a welcoming handshake. 'I was just talking about you and wondering what could be done to help you. Now here you are in my office!'

'Well,' I replied, 'I was just going past and I couldn't get rid of the thought that I needed to come and see you.'

Mr Abraham explained, 'There is a ship-building yard under my supervision on Marina Beach that has a lot of diesel engines. They need mechanical workmen. So I could send you there to work as a mechanical apprentice. You would gain practical experience and earn some money. Unfortunately, this can only be on a daily basis, though, according to the work available. I'll write to the works manager, explaining the situation.' I was overwhelmed. This was exactly what I needed.

I had already experienced provision in other areas. Two UESI staff workers, who rented a shared room two minutes away from Emmanuel Church, had invited me to live with them rent-free. I'd therefore recently moved out of my student accommodation. I'd also found out that it was possible to convert from a morning college course to an evening one so that I could undertake some gainful employment in the morning. Now, a Christian gentleman, eager to help, had thought of me and I would be a mechanical apprentice. This was very much part of my training! Everyone in Madras knows how beautiful Marina Beach is too. While it would only be on a daily basis, I called to mind Jesus' model for how we should pray: 'Give us today our daily bread' (Matthew 6:11). I couldn't believe all that had happened.

So my new routine was that I got up at about 6 a.m.; prepared my *tiffin* (packed lunch); had some breakfast; worked from 8 a.m. to 4 p.m.; cycled to evening college; studied there from 6 p.m. to 9 p.m.; came back home around 10 p.m.; ate what food was left over – if any; and fell gratefully into bed. Over a few weeks, all my cycling – from my home to the beach, from the beach to the college and from college to home – combined with insufficient nutrition (due to lack of time and money) took its toll. I collapsed while I was at work and was admitted to hospital, where I was apparently unconscious for several days. When I did eventually come round, the doctor was grave: 'You've got typhoid. If you'd been brought in any later, it would have taken your life.'

It was then that I became conscious of the faithful Madhav (Mr Giri's son-in-law) sitting at my bedside. I remained at hospital for a few more days, where the hospital staff nourished me back to health and Madhav kindly brought me extra food. He commented, 'You can't continue like this. It's not on. You are coming to stay at our house; my wife will help look after you.'

Once I was discharged, Madhav took me to Mr Giri's home. Madhav and Ratna, his wife, reassured me, 'You will stay here, and continue with your studying and doing whatever you want. You don't need to be worried about food. We will take care of you.' Once again, my heavenly Father God – as He reveals Himself in the Bible to be – impressed to me that He was more than able to take care of His children. Much later, when I came across the account of the Old Testament prophet Elijah, I was impressed by God's provision for his practical needs and recognised some parallels with my own situation.[8]

My father visits

During my stay at Mr Giri's house, in spring 1967, my dad, who would be in the vicinity with work, wanted to visit. I was concerned that my dad might arrive when I was out, so raised this with Ratna. 'But how will I recognise him?' she asked.

'Why, it will be easy,' I replied. 'Anyone who has seen me has seen the father!' I exclaimed, proudly citing a popular quote from the Bible.

A couple of days later, around lunchtime, there was a knock at the door. Ratna opened the door and, trying to suppress a giggle, addressed the man before he even had a chance to ask for me: 'Are you Bhaskar's father?'

'How did you know?' was his surprised question.

Ratna invited him in. This was natural enough as they were both Telugu speakers from a Hindu background. My dad assumed the hostess was Hindu as well. I had been anxious about him asking too many questions, in case he discover that this family were Christian and – lo and behold – so was his son. But being a man of few words, this fear was unfounded. He was instead happy that his son had seemingly found favour with a wealthy Telugu family in Madras.

For my part, I was relieved that the visit had gone ahead without any untoward happenings. I'd also been concerned that my dad might try to persuade me to go back home, but, providentially, he didn't suggest that. I wished, though, that I could have told him about my conversion there and then instead of having to wait until I was baptised a couple of months later.

Now that my dad had visited my new living conditions at Mr Giri's, and I'd reassured him that I'd definitely do my best to keep up with my studies and my health, I hoped he would take a satisfactory report home to my mum. Little would they realise, however, that this health and companionship were due entirely to my encounter with Jesus Christ.

Baptism at last

My long-awaited birthday was approaching. As promised, Pastor Kamaleson made all the necessary preparations for my baptism to go ahead on the first Sunday after my birthday. But on my actual birthday, Thursday 20 July, he phoned me at Mr Giri's house. Ostensibly this was to wish me a happy birthday, but he then asked me, 'Exactly how old are you today, Bhaskar? Are you entering your twenty-first year or are you completing your twenty-first year?'

My fears increased on hearing this question, but I managed to keep things together, responding honestly,

'I am entering my twenty-first year, Pastor. Today is my twentieth birthday.'

A moment of silence followed, after which Pastor Kamaleson said, 'I am sorry, Bhaskar, but we may have to wait for one more year as you are only twenty.'

I could feel the anger building inside me, though I could also see where he was coming from. My response was calm but indignant: 'Pastor, with due respect, I might have to ask someone else to baptise me.'

He asked for a little more time to ascertain any possible legal ramifications of conducting the baptism before I ended my twenty-first year. I agreed. He assured me that he would inform me as soon as he had any information. It seemed maddening, though, that younger men than me became fathers and drove cars, but I couldn't even be immersed in a bit of water by request.

True to his word, Pastor Kamaleson rang me back a few hours later. He had spoken to the Public Prosecutor of Madras High Court, who'd suggested that he could go ahead and baptise me provided I wrote a letter. This should state that I was undertaking baptism of my own choice, without any coercion, and that I was taking full responsibility for my own actions and decisions in this regard. Should my parents take any legal action against the pastor and the church in the future, this would safeguard them. Given the current socio-political climate in many countries, I can see the wisdom in such circumstances.

Of course, I was more than happy to accept complete responsibility for my baptism. I asked Pastor Kamaleson to compose the letter on my behalf, assuring him that I would readily sign it. But he was still hesitant. 'We will go ahead with the baptism,' he said slowly, 'provided the Lord God confirms it with the filling of the tank.'

It was now the month of July. Though it is on the coast, Madras is known to have water shortages in the summer months. In fact, water was only channelled through the municipal pipes to people's taps for a couple of hours each morning and evening. The baptism tank in the church yard, into which I'd be immersed, was very wide and very deep. The tap that would fill it was so small and so fickle that his statement wasn't an empty one. On a human level, it was virtually impossible that the tank would be filled by Sunday morning, even if the tap was left on continuously until then. Understanding what the pastor was saying, I declared, 'If the Madras water system fails, I'll ask my God to open the windows of heaven and fill it directly for me to be baptised.' He laughed when I said this, perhaps at the sheer brazenness of my new faith, or perhaps because he wanted to share my hope. This served only to make me bolder in my trust in God. We agreed on Sunday 23 July as my baptismal day.

Saturday 22 July came. There was still no rain. But during that night, Madras endured an absolute downpour – something that few apart from me were anticipating. At 4.30 in the early morning, the phone rang. It was the pastor: 'Bhaskar, the tank is overflowing! Are you ready?'

'I told you that God would supply my needs. Of course I'm ready.'

So, after seven months of disappointed waiting, Pastor Kamaleson plunged me into the overflowing baptismal tank in the church yard. Thanks to God, I was finally baptised – in front of the whole congregation of Emmanuel Methodist Church. I was elated! And very wet.

8

OUT OF THE DARKNESS

'Respected Mother and Father, greetings. I have something important to tell you. I am going to write everything in detail so that at least you might be able to start to understand what has happened to me and why ...'

The day after my baptism, Monday 24 July 1967, I composed a long letter to my parents, telling them about my change of faith. I asked them to understand that this was my own decision and tried as best I could to dampen the blow I knew they would feel.

I waited expectantly for their reply, but also with fear and trembling. Even as I posted the letter, the question that was most prominent in my mind was what I would now do with my life. It was inconceivable that my parents would accept my conversion and allow the status quo to continue regardless. It was abundantly clear that I'd have to abandon any hope of pursuing my chosen profession of engineering.

A week later, the fateful reply arrived. It consisted of two letters: one written by my dad, the other by my mum. My dad's was straightforward and to the point: 'Unless you renounce this madness, all my support will stop. You will have to work out for yourself how you will survive in Madras.' From that day onwards, our relationship was irreversibly fractured; my dad no longer regarded me as his son. To my sorrow, it stayed like this until his dying day.

My mum's letter was more emotional. Stating that I was the best-loved of her six children, she asked, 'Why are you ignoring my love and all that I have showered upon you since you were born?' She then warned me, 'If you continue in this faith, I'll be left with no choice but to consider you as dead to me.' This hurt me deeply, but the love and acceptance I had in Jesus Christ were worth any price, however painful.

As often happens when a Hindu becomes a follower of Jesus Christ, I was disowned and disinherited by my parents. In practice, I'd become an orphan overnight. They instantly cut off all my funding and support, leaving me simply with the clothes I'd brought to university – and a whole load of vexing questions like where I would live, what would become of my future career and how I would even survive.

Doubt and fear could have easily prevailed here, but, for the third time, these song words came ringing in my ears: 'I have decided to follow Jesus ... no turning back, no turning back.'

Akka

It wasn't until some years later that I was able to explain face-to-face to Akka what had happened, though she had obviously found out from the family their version of events. When I finally met her, the first thing I did was to present her with a small gift of two pieces of white fabric. 'No one ever did anything like this for me,' Akka exclaimed, visibly moved. But then, after a short pause, she asked, 'Why is it that you broke all ties of affection with me and your family, and became a Christian? Do you even think about me at all? Why did you do this to me?'

I'd experienced the pain of losing my relationship with my family, exacerbated by a pressing concern for their souls that every Christian should be able to identify with. Now to face my beloved and bereft Akka was almost too much to bear. But I answered her honestly. 'I miss you, Akka, and I think about you often. No one can ever take your place in my life.'

'Then why did you leave all of us, and especially me? You know I have nobody except you,' she pointed out.

'Let me ask you, Akka, why have you suffered so much and are still suffering so much?'

The reply was well-rehearsed. 'It is because of my evil karma, Bhaskar, in my past incarnations and in this life.'

'Is it going to take a long time for you to remove your bad karma, Akka?'

'You know it will take a very long time indeed, Bhaskar. I am the worst when it comes to evil karma.'

I grasped the opportunity to share something of the gospel of Jesus. 'If someone cancels all your evil karma and gives you 100 per cent good karma instead, will you be reborn again into another incarnation?'

She sneered. 'No, of course not. I'll be full of bliss and happiness.' After a pause, she added, 'But that is not possible, Bhaskar. So I suffer and will continue to suffer. That is just how it is.'

'You asked me why I became a Christian. It's because the Lord Jesus Christ has performed a wonderful transaction: He has paid the debt of all my evil karma and in its place He has credited me with His own 100 per cent goodness.'

She remarked, 'If that is the case, I am happy for you. Continue in that life.'

Her reaction may surprise some readers. Why didn't Akka ask for this gracious transaction for herself? I've found over the years that even though my family and others can see and understand on a rational level the power, love and merciful offer of Jesus Christ, they aren't interested in having it for themselves. Their attitude is exemplified in what my mum said to me many years later: 'You can have it, Bhaskar, but we don't want it. We know your God is more powerful than ours and answers your prayers, but we will follow our way.' It seems that the social or family stigma of becoming a Christian is too great for them to consider it themselves.

The Bible also teaches that the faith and strength to decide to follow Christ can come only from God Himself.

Once, my mum asked me, 'Can I follow Jesus Christ without calling myself a Christian?'

I answered, 'If you follow Christ, whether you call yourself a Christian or not, the fact is you are a Christian!'

'I love Christ, but I dislike Christians,' was her matter-of-fact reply. Sadly, to the best of my knowledge, my mother didn't ever accept the offer to follow Christ.

Years later, my mum and my brother Krishna unfairly, but inevitably, accused Mr Giri's family of pressurising me to become a Christian. They wouldn't accept any other explanation. It was impossible to convince them that I'd met Mr Giri only after becoming a Christian. Even today, the general consensus in India is that conversion can only take place due to external pressure or coercion from so-called missionaries, or is chosen to escape the oppression of belonging to a low caste. I also think my mum preferred to blame someone else for my conversion than to accept that I'd chosen such a drastic course of action by my own will.

From engineering college to Bible college

As for my anxieties about how I'd survive without my family, I needn't have been concerned. My heavenly Father was already moving the machinery of earth and heaven to supply my needs in accordance with His perfect will.

But for the first two or three weeks, I was in limbo. My parents had closed the door to me pursuing an engineering career; a new door to something else was not yet opened. Even then, my needs were still being met – physically through the generosity of Mr Giri; spiritually by God Himself, through His own presence with me, His people and His church.

A place I kept hearing about at Emmanuel Methodist Church was Yavatmal, specifically a Bible college there. I presumed it to be in another country far, far away, as I'd never heard of it before. I felt secretly sad that I wouldn't be able to go to what sounded like a good Bible college. But one day, when I was at home, flicking through a Christian magazine, a small advert in the corner of the page caught my eye. It was for Union Bible Seminary, Yavatmal, Maharashtra. Maharashtra was in India; this meant that Yavatmal Bible College was in India as well! So, without telling anyone else, I sent off for an application form.

My excitement was short-lived: when I saw how high the fees were, I thought that it would actually be easier to fund the engineering degree than this Christian training course! Not entirely deterred, though, I noticed that there were various funding options, including full and part bursaries. Either way, a necessary requirement of the application form was the signature of my pastor.

When I took it to Pastor Kamaleson, I asked his advice about which tier of funding to apply for. He smiled and stated that all I needed to do was write on the dotted line: 'Emmanuel Methodist Church'. Seeing that I was perplexed at this, he explained, 'Don't you understand, Bhaskar? The young people's fellowship has been praying for someone to sponsor to send to Yavatmal.' Unbeknown to me, a group of God's faithful followers in Emmanuel had been earnestly praying that God would raise up a young man to go to Bible College, who they could support in giving and praying. They had been pleased to send their first-ever student to a Bible College recently, and now sought God's will to send another. 'You are the answer to their prayers,' continued Pastor Kamaleson. 'They will pay all your expenses.'

I was flabbergasted. I was the answer to their prayers? Rather, they were the answer to mine.

And so the story of my conversion ends – as most people's do – with a new beginning.

EPILOGUE

The L<small>ORD</small> is my shepherd, I lack nothing …
He guides me along the right paths
for his name's sake.
Even though I walk
through the darkest valley,
I will fear no evil,
for you are with me.

(Psalm 23:1–4)

This psalm, or song, is one of the most famous passages in the Bible. It declares that God leads His people in paths of righteousness 'for his name's sake'. I can testify that this is what He has done for me in many astonishing ways. Notably, in the early days of my becoming a Christian, He opened the door for me to go to Bible college, where incidentally I also met my wife-to-be, and He gave me a whole new calling – not as an engineer, but as an evangelist, telling others the good news about Jesus.

'For his name's sake' is the reason my daughter-in-law and I have written this book. We wanted to share with you the marvellous testimony of how the God of the Bible – the God of the Universe, the One who 'knit me together in my mother's womb' (Psalm 139:13) – answered my deep and heartfelt desire to know the truths of eternity. He knew me, rescued me, saved me.

It would take a whole other book to tell you just some of the amazing ways God provided for me and some of the loving people He brought into my life. My life as a Christian hasn't always been easy, but it has always been blessed. My desire is that through reading the story of me, an Indian boy, you too may know the freedom from fear that comes from knowing Jesus Christ, and the peace that is derived from knowing that your life *and* your eternity are in His hands. All my previous efforts to obtain *moksha* were ineffectual and only resulted in futile frustration. It is Jesus' grace, Jesus' works, Jesus' holiness, Jesus' merits, Jesus' efforts and Jesus' blood that have paid for my salvation, and He can pay for yours as well.

A verse from the Bible that has motivated me throughout my adult life is John 17:3: 'Now this is eternal life: that they know you, the only true God, and Jesus Christ, whom you have sent.' I came to know this truth after many years of seeking in the wrong place. I hope I have shown you, through this small book, where to find eternal life which is better than *moksha*.

God's work in my life didn't stop the day I became a Christian or even the day I was baptised. It will continue until my last moment on this earth. But even that is just the beginning because afterwards, I know that I shall enjoy being in His presence in heaven, where time does not exist.

How long will you try to earn your own salvation by pursuing meaningless actions and rituals? Christ alone has paid for the salvation of all who accept Him exclusively as Lord and God.

POSTSCRIPT
BY ESTHER SANDYS

*... all the days ordained for me were written in your book
before one of them came to be.*

(Psalm 139:16)

Just before his seventieth birthday, in July 2017, Bhaskar died as a result of a respiratory complication. His earthly work done, the Lord took him home. Although to those who knew him this was unexpected, Psalm 139:16 tells us that all our days are numbered by the Lord.

The timing of Bhaskar's call home (as Christians often refer to the passing from physical life into eternal life) was striking and blessed in several ways. Two factors were especially notable. Firstly, we had already finished drafting this book recording God's faithfulness. Secondly, a key part of Bhaskar's ministry was being pastor of the Bristol Asian Christian Fellowship in the UK. Five months before the

Lord called him home, the fellowship marked its twenty-fifth anniversary with a special recognition of Bhaskar's leadership. Providentially, a godly and able man had been raised up by this time to take over from Bhaskar. All this reminded his family and friends that God is in control.

Reflecting on Bhaskar's life and death, I can't help thinking about how they differed from his great-uncle's terrifying and distressing last moments on earth. On Bhaskar's death bed, his last words were calm and willing. With his hand raised, gazing into the distance, Bhaskar responded to his Saviour's call with, 'I am coming'. He was finally going home to be with his Lord!

The only way to have peace with God in this life and at death is to surrender yourself to the Lord Jesus Christ. He loves you unconditionally, since before your creation. He died for you, thus paying the punishment for your sin, so that you are no longer under God's righteous judgement. In Him you can be absolutely assured of release from sorrow and enjoy the presence of the Lord for all eternity in heaven.

Won't you come to Him today?

NOTES

1. Incidentally, although attitudes today towards dowries are mixed, they became more prominent following India's independence from the British colonisers in 1947 because of a desire to be identified as an Indian, Hindu, non-British, non-Islamic nation.

2. Over the last few decades, however, a sluggish change in this attitude has begun, thanks in part to influential Bollywood films such as *Sholay* (1975), *Prem Rog* (1982) and *Baabul* (2006).

3. According to this story, Prahlad was born to a notoriously wicked king who had arrogantly claimed that he alone was the supreme god. However, his mother had enjoyed the privilege of learning from a renowned Hindu teacher. Therefore, the boy grew up to be more devoted and religious than his arrogant father. He was young but pious. When he challenged his father's claim, he inadvertently caused his father's death by an incarnation of Vishnu.

4. Another reason for this was that I admired the bravery and determination shown by a boy called Markandeya. In *Markandeya Purana*, the boy Markandeya is told that he will die on his sixteenth birthday. He asks his parents who would be able to help him escape an early death. They respond that Shiva could help. So, before midnight of his sixteenth birthday, Markandeya goes into the temple of Shiva and holds on to his iconic statue, the Shivalinga, all night long. Just before dawn, the god of death, Yama, comes to take his life away, but Markandeya won't let go of the Shivalinga. Very soon, Shiva appears, drives Yama away and grants the boy long life.

5. Taken from the hymn 'O my heart is full of gladness since by faith I saw the Lord' by Alfred Barratt.

6. Taken from the hymn 'I have decided to follow Jesus', attributed to Sadhu Sundar Singh.

7. You can read about this in Matthew 3:13–17.

8. God's provision for Elijah can be found in 1 Kings 17.

10Publishing is the publishing house of **10ofThose**.
It is committed to producing quality Christian resources
that are biblical and accessible.

www.10ofthose.com is our online retail arm selling
thousands of quality books at discounted prices.

For information contact: **info@10ofthose.com**
or check out our website: **www.10ofthose.com**